S23 .

SIS

Therapists in Court

Legal Resources for Counsellors and Psychotherapists

Legal Resources for Counsellors and Psychotherapists is a series of highly practical books, themed around broad topics, which reflect the most 'frequently asked questions' put to the BACP's professional advice line.

Therapists in Court

Providing Evidence and Supporting Witnesses

British Association for
Counselling and Psychotherapy

Tim Bond and Amanpreet Sandhu

Los Angeles | London | New Delhi
Singapore | Washington DC

First published 2005
Reprinted 2009, 2010

SAGE Publications Ltd
1 Oliver's Yard
55 City Road
London EC1Y 1SP

SAGE Publications Inc.
2455 Teller Road
Thousand Oaks, California 91320

SAGE Publications India Pvt Ltd
B 1/I 1 Mohan Cooperative Industrial Area
Mathura Road
New Delhi 110 044

SAGE Publications Asia-Pacific Pte Ltd
33 Pekin Street #02-01
Far East Square
Singapore 048763

British Library Cataloguing in Publication data

A catalogue record for this book is
available from the British Library

ISBN 978-1-4129-1267-9
ISBN 978-1-4129-1268-6

Library of Congress Control Number: 2005926166

Typeset by C&M Digitals (P) Ltd., Chennai, India
Printed on paper from sustainable resources
Printed in Great Britain by Ashford Colour Press Ltd

Contents

Preface

This book is the first in a series of legal guidance handbooks for practitioners from all the talking therapies, including counselling, psychotherapy and psychology. The talking therapies are a significant and growing source of support in contemporary society. A recent national survey revealed that 1 in 5 of the adult population in the UK have personally received counselling or psychotherapy and 83 per cent of those surveyed stated that they would consider having this type of service.[1] This indicates a substantial volume of actual and potential activity within society. It is inevitable that in the process of providing this service on such a large scale, practitioners will come into contact with the law. This can lead practitioners to experience anxiety, especially if their first formal encounter is being called as a witness or they are asked to write a report for the unfamiliar settings and procedures of a court.

For many practitioners, becoming involved in a court case is a frightening and disturbing experience. Competent and experienced practitioners will have become familiar with a very different environment in their work. Therapy is predominantly characterised by privacy, informality and attentiveness to the quality of relationship with clients, in order to enhance the therapeutic effectiveness. In contrast, the court room is usually a public place and may have press reporters present. Typically, the atmosphere is formal and much more attentive to bureaucratic detail than to the quality of relationships between those present. Witnesses are particularly vulnerable in these unfamiliar settings.

Although courts strive to be respectful of witnesses, their experience can be unpredictable and may range from supportive questioning to verbal bullying in cross examination. I have heard many therapists talk of their shock at finding that their work has taken them into such an adversarial environment leaving them feeling perplexed, uncertain and frequently misunderstood. This sense of misunderstanding often arises from a sense that the court is disinterested in the practitioner's area of expertise in therapeutic issues. Instead, many practitioners feel that they have been summoned to court to be targeted with questions by lawyers in pursuit of evidence to be used for legal objectives, over which the therapist has little control or knowledge. At its worst, I have known practitioners find that the experience undermines their confidence as professionals and they are left deeply concerned that they may have inadvertently or been forced into situations where they have damaged any therapeutic good that has been achieved for the client concerned, prior to the court appearance. Even in more favourable situations, practitioners frequently find that their involvement in any legal process disrupts their therapeutic relationships with the affected clients.

The best way of avoiding or at least minimising the negative aspects of appearing in court is to be competently informed and prepared in advance. Legal textbooks provide some essential information but often this is at more theoretical level than is helpful to professionals from other disciplines. In my experience, practitioners often want very practical information as the starting point in orientating themselves towards a new environment and professional culture. As practitioners become better informed, they become empowered to take greater control of the situation. This book is intended to support this process of becoming better informed. In the adversarial environment of most courtrooms, to be forewarned is to be forearmed.

Although I am aware of some negative experiences which therapists have faced arising from court cases concerning their clients, this is neither inevitable or invariably the case. At the other extreme some therapists have found the experience to be professionally and personally rewarding. Supporting witnesses in their preparation to appear in court or working with clients where the practitioner knows that there is the likelihood of being called as a witness can be viewed as an opportunity to make distinctive contribution to clients' lives and to the delivery of justice in society. There are a small but growing number of forensic therapists who specialise in undertaking independent psychological assessments for the courts and counselling the victims or perpetrators of crimes and civil wrongs.

Amanpreet Sandhu has drawn on her experience as legal resource manager in a professional body to produce information that will be of direct help to both reluctant and willing participants in the courts of the English, Welsh and Northern Irish legal systems. Some of the general principles are directly applicable to the Scottish legal system although there are differences in detail and terminology. These differences have been included whenever possible throughout the series.

As series editor, I have become profoundly aware of the difficulty of encompassing the range of relevant law for practitioners providing such different services in such a wide range of settings. This book is a valuable contribution to that task and significantly extends the available literature. Although the book is as legally accurate as possible at the time of going to press, the law will continue to develop concerning most of its topics. If something is of substantial significance to you or your client, there is no substitute for obtaining up-to-date advice on the specific circumstances of your issue from an appropriately qualified and experienced lawyer.

Tim Bond
Reader in Counselling and Professional Ethics
University of Bristol

---

1 The Future Foundation (2004) *The Age of Therapy: Exploring Attitudes towards and Acceptance of Counselling and Psychotherapy in Modern Britain*. Rugby: British Association for Counselling and Psychotherapy. Page 3

Acknowledgements

The authors of this book and BACP would like to offer their thanks to and acknowledge the following people who have contributed to the various chapters in this book.

Len Tempest contributed to the chapter Solicitor Letters. Len is a practising barrister.

Angela Churm contributed to the chapter Court Orders. Angela is an experienced practitioner who progressed from a legal background where she undertook extensive work in the court system, and is also an experienced writer.

David Trickey contributed to the chapter Counselling Child Witnesses. David is a Chartered Clinical Psychologist and, at the time of writing, was based in the Child and Family Team at the Traumatic Stress Clinic in London.

Ruth Harrison contributed to the chapter Counselling Adult Victims and Witnesses. Ruth has considerable experience in counselling, specifically offering counselling support to victims and their families, who have been involved in major transport accidents such as the Potters Bar and Paddington train crashes. Ruth also does some work for the Nursing and Midwifery Council.

We are grateful to Roisin Higgins for highlighting the relevant Scottish law in each instance. Special thanks also go to Kirstie Adamson for her contributions to the chapter Counselling Adult Victims and Witnesses. The Criminal Injury Compensation Authority also deserves a special mention for allowing BACP permission to reproduce a standard *pro forma* report that it uses as part of its investigations.

Introduction

'A solicitor has written to me demanding all my notes about one of my clients.
Do I have to send them?'

'I have been approached to counsel a very anxious 10-year-old-girl who is
waiting to appear as witness in a child abuse case. She has changed from
happy outward-going girl to someone who is withdrawn at home and school.
She is just the witness, not the victim. Can I counsel her?'

'My client has asked me to provide a report to help him in a case where he
is suing someone following an accident. I am not sure that this is something
that I should be doing as therapist. Can he compel me to produce a report?
If he can force me to do this, what should I be saying?'

'I have been ordered by court to appear as witness. I think that this
will completely disrupt the therapy with my client. We have discussed
her personal relationships in confidence and it seems wrong to break this
understanding and discuss them in a court with her relatives and
the public present. Do I have to do this?'

'I have been asked to provide a report about my work with my client for a
case concerning who looks after the children following a bitter separation.
I can say quite a lot in her favour but I also know things that could work
against her. Do I have to reveal these?'

These types of enquires are increasingly commonplace in the world of therapy. Counsellors, psychotherapists and psychologists are increasingly being contacted by lawyers and the courts to provide information about their work. They are also likely to be working with clients who are involved with court cases as witnesses or victims. Few therapists feel adequately trained or sufficiently experienced to be confident about how to respond to these situations. Many are justifiably concerned about how to manage the different expectations of legal and therapeutic processes.

This series has been written to meet the growing demand from therapists for advice about situations in which their therapeutic work as counsellors, psychotherapists and psychologists brings them into contact with the law. Therapists often report difficulty in finding information that relates to their professional field. The obvious sources of information are either not detailed enough to be of practical use or so technically complex that they are only understood by trained lawyers. This is clearly unsatisfactory and exposes both clients and therapists to unnecessary and probably avoidable legal risks. All professional bodies require their practitioners to know the law that relates to their field of practice and we hope that this series will make this requirement easier to achieve.

All the books in this series are designed to identify those areas of law that impinge on therapeutic practice and to provide relevant information in as user friendly way as possible for therapists. As authors, we have worked as a team. Amanpreet Sandhu has used her experience as a legal resource manager in the British Association for Counselling and Psychotherapy to identify, clarify and set out relevant areas of law. Tim Bond has drawn on his experience in professional ethics and conduct, especially his experience of advising practitioners, to generate practical examples of the application of the law to therapeutic practice and to ask questions about the law from a therapist's perspective. The books cannot be a substitute for obtaining good up-to-date legal advice on specific matters of importance. However, they are intended to alert therapists to potential difficulties or opportunities in the legal aspects of their work. Prior knowledge of the relevant law places therapists in the best possible position to plan systems for delivering their services to take advantage of the protection offered by the law and to anticipate any potential problems. A working knowledge of the law also enables therapists to ask more relevant and better informed questions when seeking legal advice.

The structure of this book

As the first book of the series, we decided that it would be appropriate to consider the source of some of the most urgent and anguished queries about what to do when either a client or a therapist becomes involved in litigation. This creates the immediate prospect of therapists being brought face-to-face with the law at its most intimidating and magisterial in the courts. It is only the exceptional therapist who has any previous experience of the involvement of their cases with the law. Unlike social workers and probation officers, few therapists have had any training in the trail of paperwork that precedes most cases, appearing as a witness or writing professional reports for use by lawyers. They are also seldom prepared to take into account the implications of a client seeking therapy who is involved in litigation whether as a witness in a criminal case or as a party to civil action. This book considers some of the more commonly occurring situations and is structured around these.

The first section, 'Therapists entering the legal process', considers how they can become directly involved in legal cases that may end up in court. It provides essential legal information to answer questions about:

- Responding to solicitors' letters.
- Court orders concerning the production of documents or appearance as a witness.
- Writing reports with examples of all the more common types of reports.
- Presenting your work as a witness in court.
- Fees and expenses for work connected with the law.

The second section considers the challenges of 'Working with clients involved in the law' and particularly issues concerning working with:

- Child witnesses, especially victims.
- Adult victims and witnesses.
- Criminal compensation claims for physical and psychological injuries.

The final chapter provides useful information about the different types of courts within the United Kingdom and their functions, including the different roles of people within the legal system. Sufficient information is given for therapists to find their way round the English and Scottish legal systems.

Using this book

All therapists face the possibility of being drawn into the legal process at some time or another. For most, this involvement with the law will be an exceptional experience that arises, sometimes unexpectedly, due to the unusual circumstances of a particular client. Most therapists working in private practice or voluntary agencies with a general range of clients, report that they are only occasionally caught up in legal processes connected with their clients. However, it is increasingly commonplace for therapists working in the health service, education, or services supporting families to receive regular legal inquires, with some requiring substantial further involvement. Responding to legal inquiries may even be routine for services involved in supporting victims or offenders.

Whether or not therapists are occasionally or regularly involved in legal processes, familiarising yourself with the contents of this book in general terms is advisable so that you have a sense of what involvement with the law might mean for your work with clients; it will put therapists in the best possible position to respond to requests from clients about legal matters. It may also assist therapists to identify cases where future legal involvement is more probable than others. Therapists working with any of the following should consider the possibility of unavoidable legal involvement at some future date:

- Anyone who has suffered physical or psychological trauma arising from an accident or crime.
- Clients who make the first report of sexual assault to their therapist as this is likely to be regarded as crucial evidence in any subsequent prosecution.
- Members of families in dispute about the care and custody of children.
- Vulnerable young people.
- Clients who commit suicide.

Therapists working with clients in any of these categories are well-advised to develop a detailed knowledge of the relevant law and associated legal processes. The books in this series are designed to be useful points of reference for detailed legal information relevant to the development and delivery of these kinds of services. These books are also intended to be a useful first point of reference, in the event of the therapist becoming legally involved in a specific case, so that he or she is better able to seek appropriate legal advice.

A valuable feature of this book is the inclusion of examples showing the types of documents therapists might be asked to produce. These documents are realistic; they are based on the types of documents and statements presented in actual cases. However, the details about the actual events and people concerned are fictional in order to avoid compromising the anonymity of any clients or the integrity of actual cases. The examples are written in a variety of styles to indicate how varied legal documents can be. They provide examples of how to address a concern that carries less weight in therapy than in law.

The primary focus of most therapy is subjective experience where inner experience is paid more attention than external events. The therapist's trained intuition is a valid source of information and the basis for action in therapy. Intuition is of much lower standing in law and is often treated with suspicion. Lawyers tend to approach human experience in a very different way. Their practice is shaped by working in a context where there are often conflicting accounts of events or interpretations of the events. As a consequence, lawyers tend to be more concerned with separating identifying facts and separating facts from opinion. The first step in any legal process is usually to determine the facts from the available evidence by a combination of scientific and logical reasoning. Only once the available facts have been determined will attention be turned to the possible interpretations of those facts and considering which interpretation is the most appropriate professional or legal opinion. Therapists are therefore not only faced with the need for technical knowledge about the way the law is applied to their work but they are also encountering a different mindset and way of thinking when they come into contact with legal processes. The examples of representative documents have been developed to provide insight into the challenges of presenting therapeutic work within a legal context. Many of them are also interesting reading in their own right and may persuade some therapists that overcoming the difficulties of presenting their work for lawyers is a worthwhile endeavour in the interests of their clients and also the well-being of society. It is certainly a professional and personal challenge.

At the end of the book there is also a glossary for readers. It is a useful reference tool for any legalistic terminology that you are unsure about.

The book opens with what is probably the most common starting point for therapists' involvement with the law, the arrival of a letter from a solicitor.

Part One

Therapists entering the legal process

Solicitor Letters

The sight of an official-looking envelope from a solicitor peering out from under a pile of junk mail is enough to instil a sense of fear and trepidation among most therapists. A common first reaction is to open the letter with the intention of complying fully with what is being requested. The solicitor headed paper, official tone of the contents, and the authoritative demands made, are all designed to play on the reader's anxiety that any refusal to comply will mean some kind of legal reprimand or lead them to being hauled up in front of the judge. Lawyers know their letters can be intimidating to the lay person. They are not above using scare tactics in order to extract all the available information that will assist them with their client's case. Lawyers often implicitly encourage the mistaken belief in therapists that they have no choice but to comply with their requests. The reality is somewhat different. Except in the limited circumstances discussed in this chapter, there is no overriding duty to respond or divulge any information at the mere request of a solicitor's letter. Understanding the motives behind such letters and their function in the legal process will help you to avoid taking impulsive actions when responding to a solicitor's letter. This chapter encourages you to take a step back and consider all the relevant factors before responding.

There are three situations in which a therapist could receive a letter from a solicitor:

1   *Where the client intends to take action against a third party*: Anne is suffering from post-traumatic stress disorder as a result of experiencing sexual harassment at work and would like her therapist to disclose notes for the purpose of bringing an action against her employers.
2   *Where the third party intends to take action against the client. This is most likely to occur where the police are in the process of conducting an investigation*: The police have been investigating Anne for some time and believe she may have sold some of her assets for the purpose of financing a terrorist act. The police will want disclosure from the therapist in pursuit of their investigation.
3   *Where the client intends to take action against the therapist*: Anne believes that her therapist has not offered her the correct therapeutic treatment and that her health has deteriorated even more as a direct consequence of this. She is bringing an action in professional negligence against her therapist.

The most frequent source of correspondence concerns the first of these situations and is therefore considered first within this chapter.

Responding to a letter where a client intends to take action against a third party

This is perhaps one of the most common ways in which a therapist will come into contact with the law. For example, they may have been counselling a client suffering from post-traumatic stress following a road traffic accident. It is quite probable in such cases that the client will be pursuing a claim for injury and his or her solicitor may contact the therapist for any relevant information in support of such a claim. Sometimes the therapist will have been alerted to this possibility by the client themselves who will often disclose that they are considering suing an individual who has caused them harm. However, these letters can arise unexpectedly, particularly in relation to former clients. Many solicitors use a standard format for these letters. The following is a typical example:

Dear Ms Offer

Re: Ann Bloggs

We are instructed by our above-named client whom we understand is a client at your practice.
  We are preparing our client's claim for personal injury arising out of an accident that occurred on 15 October 2004.
  We should be grateful if you would supply us with a complete copy of your client notes and records.
  We are of course prepared to pay your reasonable charges in accordance with the Data Protection Act (Subject Access) (Fees 7 Miscellaneous Provision) Regulations.
  Please find enclosed a copy of our client's signed medical authority form. You will note that no proceedings are contemplated against your practice or against the health authority.

We look forward to hearing from you.

Yours sincerely

Mills & Sterling Solicitors

However the letter is worded it will usually include a statement and evidence that the request is being made with the client's permission. This is intended to reassure the therapist that the request is being made with the client's knowledge and full support, in order to alleviate any concerns over confidentiality. However, it is not unreasonable for the therapist to contact the client to ensure that they understand the implications of this request and that they are giving full and informed consent.

There is also usually reference to the Data Protection Act 1998. This reference is commonly used to inform the therapist that the client is legally entitled to the information and that the therapist has a legal obligation to provide it. This was widely accepted as good law until a recent development in common law. The distinctive feature of the 1998 legislation had been to extend data protection principles from electronic records to all types of records including manual records, such as case notes. The current state of the law is more complex than this, following *Durant* v. *Financial Services Authority* 2003. The practical implications of these recent legal developments are that the client's right to insist on access to his or her records is currently restricted to those that are held electronically or have been made on behalf of a public service, such as education, health and social services (Freedom of Information Act 2000). Clients who have been receiving services in any other context no longer have a legal entitlement to their handwritten records. In the absence of any legal duty to disclose records to clients, therapists are entitled to use their own judgement in deciding whether to disclose records in response to this type of letter. This is fundamentally an ethical decision to be made in accordance with the ethical principles that inform your work.

The precise content of a letter from the solicitor can vary considerably. The second example illustrates how important it is to read the letter carefully:

Accident: Ann Bloggs on 15 October 2004

We act for the above-named Client in connection with a claim for compensation for personal injuries and financial loss suffered as a result of an accident, which occurred on the aforesaid date.

   We would be grateful if you could forward to us, as soon as possible, our Client's counselling records or copies of the same and we enclose a Form of Authority authorising disclosure of the above documents.

   Please note that we confirm that we shall pay your reasonable administration/ photocopying charges.

Yours faithfully

Mills & Sterling Solicitors

The significant features of this letter are firstly, there is no statement or evidence that the request for information has been initiated at the client's request. A conscientious therapist would certainly want to clarify this issue with the solicitor and most probably the client before making any decision on how to respond. Secondly, there is no explicit or implicit reference to any legal obligation to provide information. The wording and tone of the letter suggest that the decision about how to respond rests with the therapist.

How should therapists deal with the initial contact from a solicitor?

It is good practice for therapists to give careful consideration to any request for information from a solicitor. Where the first contact is by telephone, it is reasonable to ask the solicitor to put his or her request in writing, unless the solicitor is following up something that you have already agreed with your client to your own satisfaction. If the therapist is satisfied that there is no legal obligation to provide this information, they may simply ignore the request or perhaps, more professionally, simply respond stating that they do not intend to supply the requested information. In some instances the information may have already been destroyed as part of good data protection practice. Where this is the case the solicitor should be informed that these records no longer exist. In some instances no records will have been made and again the solicitor should be informed.

Where the therapist is uncertain about either their legal obligations or how best to respond to the initial letter, it is quite reasonable to ask for further information.

Making a request for further information

Therapists can in effect 'turn the tables' on the solicitor, by asking the solicitor to provide further or full information in support of the request for information. They can request any of the following, which has not been provided adequately in the original request:

- Confirmation and proof that the client has authorised disclosure of requested information.
- Details of the solicitors making the request and who they are representing.
- Precise details of what information they are asking to be disclosed.
- Why they are asking for disclosure of the information.
- Within what time scales the information is required.
- What assurances can be given about any subsequent use of the information provided.

When all relevant information has been obtained from the solicitor, the therapist is then in a position to make an informed decision about the next steps to take. The therapist is also able to demonstrate that proper care has been taken and that any decision regarding disclosure has been made conscientiously. The opportunity to obtain further information is sometimes restricted by the solicitor's willingness or ability to respond to the therapist's questions. In this case, the therapist is faced with making a decision on the available evidence or, if the matter is of such fundamental concern, refusing to make a decision until the information is provided. There have been instances where the initial request for information has been made at extremely short notice, for example within three days of a court or tribunal hearing. In these circumstances the therapist may wish to obtain the additional information by telephone, to be confirmed later in writing, in order to make an adequately informed decision. Where the therapist is feeling unduly pressurised, either by the demanding, authoritative tone of a letter or by the pressure of short time limits, it is advisable to obtain independent legal and/or professional advice. Obtaining independent advice is widely accepted as good practice before responding to any request for information, unless the therapist is satisfied about the basis for the request. It is virtually impossible to retrieve information once it is disclosed, so this decision is critical both to the therapeutic relationship and to the legal proceedings.

How do some therapists respond to a typical request from a solicitor?

In order to establish how some therapists would respond to requests from solicitors about their clients, a typical case scenario was developed by Caroline Jones as part of a regular feature of the *Counselling and Psychotherapy Journal* (*CPJ*) produced by BACP (Bond et al., 2001: 6–8). Although the original article suggested three different ways to respond to the request from the solicitors, the response in the example below has been adapted to provide a single, all-encompassing approach to the example at hand. The response is tailored to the specific scenario. However, there are also some general principles relating to responding to a solicitor's letter, which therapists can take away with them.

John came for counselling with Maria several months after he experienced a traumatic incident at work. Since the incident he has been on sick leave and is being treated by his GP for anxiety and depression. The symptoms he presented include flashbacks, nightmares, lack of confidence, withdrawal from his social network and increased smoking and drinking – all symptoms associated with post-traumatic stress disorder. After a number of sessions, which John is finding helpful, he informs Maria that he is suing his employers. Shortly before the next session Maria receives a letter from his solicitors requesting that she passes her complete, original case file to them to assist in the case. Written consent from John is enclosed with the request.

Maria's primary concern is working with John to help him overcome the trauma as quickly as possible. Whether or not John expressed an intention to sue for damages, she needs to be mindful of this possibility from the outset and consider raising it at an appropriate point in their counselling sessions. Although it would be ideal for their work to continue independently of any legal proceedings, it would be unrealistic to assume that this would be the case. Current legal practice places great emphasis on disclosure of all potentially relevant evidence in civil proceedings of this kind, in the interests of enhancing justice for everyone involved in the case.

Upon receiving the letter from the solicitor, Maria should not panic. First and foremost she needs to consider the request against the ethical principles that guide her practice. These requests often raise complex issues, which may be about trust, respecting the client's autonomy, promoting the client's well-being, avoiding harm to the client, providing justice and the therapist's own entitlement to self-respect. Maria may also want to consider the implications for herself in terms of the potential risks of complying or refusing to comply with the request. However, in relation to the client's interests, these considerations would often be secondary to the decision-making process. Bearing all of this in mind, Maria then needs to give careful consideration to the request in order to decide what action will be the most helpful to her client and to ensure that she does nothing that will harm her client or be detrimental to his interests. Maria's first actions should therefore be to:

- Obtain all the relevant information from the solicitor.
- Review the case file and consider its contents in relation to the request. For example, identify whether it contains anything particularly sensitive, bearing in mind that any disclosures in counselling can become available to all parties to the case and be used in ways which are unpredictable and may be detrimental to John.
- Contact her professional indemnity insurance company for advice.
- Consult with her supervisor and line manager (if relevant) to clarify the organisational policy on this issue.
- Go through the file with John to check that his consent to its release is fully informed. Maria should seek to make John aware that although John's solicitor has a duty of confidentiality to her client, once information from the file is used in legal proceedings, the other party may access all the information. She needs to ensure that John realises that the notes may have to be made available to his employers through their solicitors, and that she has no control over how widely they may be circulated and how they might be interpreted. In this case, John has given written consent for his case file to be released. However, if John does not know what information it contains, Maria would need to consider how 'informed' his consent is. She should seek to ensure that John is in agreement with her in providing information to his solicitor. If, as a result he is in any doubt, she should support him in taking his own time to decide.

Maria may decide that she is not prepared to hand over her complete case file. In this instance, she could suggest two alternatives to John:

- The possibility of providing a brief report on her work with him and the problems and issues that he has presented. Once the content has been agreed, he can then give this to his solicitor.
- Encourage John to seek an independent assessment of his degree of post-traumatic stress from a competent chartered psychologist or psychiatrist who specialises in this type of work. This type of assessment is not within Maria's range of competence or interest and its existence and the accompanying report would reduce the focus on her records and opinions. The author of the report may require access to her records. Her records are required to be factually accurate about any reported symptoms associated with the trauma and the originating cause. This information needs to be clarified with John as appropriate.

To summarise, on receipt of the solicitor's letter, it is good practice for Maria to discuss the above matters with John, if she has not already done so, and to check that he is aware of what he is consenting to and the potential implications for their work. John's involvement in the decision will usually reduce or clarify any ethical concerns. Maria needs to bear in mind that, as a result of providing her notes, she may then be called as a witness by either side.

Responding to a letter from a solicitor acting on behalf of a third party

A situation may occur where a therapist receives a letter from a solicitor acting on behalf of a third party who intends to take action against a client, and requests the therapist's client notes. The defendant may have been receiving therapy either prior to or during the trial and the sole purpose of the request would be to gain access to any adverse information that may have been disclosed in the therapy room. There is no obligation to respond to or disclose any notes to the prosecutor in these circumstances. For example, if therapists respond to such a speculative request from a prosecutor, any response they make could confirm that the client is someone who has received therapy. This could potentially be a breach of confidentiality, unless the information is disclosed with the client's consent or disclosure is legally required. There are only two ways in which disclosure can be compelled in these cases:

- Through a witness summons/citation compelling therapists to come to court, bringing with them the relevant documents stated in the summons.
- Through a court order (see Chapter 2).

Responding to a letter where the client instructs a solicitor on taking action against the therapist

The third and final circumstance in which a therapist may receive a letter from a solicitor is where a client, usually an ex-client, is intending to bring an action to sue the therapist. This is a rare event, especially for those therapists whose work is informed by good professional and legal practice. However, living in an increasingly litigious society, where individuals are becoming more aware of the potential rewards from litigation, such actions may become more common. Frequently, these cases do not reach the courts, as they do not get past the initial investigation. Even if these actions are not followed through to a trial, the recipient of such a letter from the solicitor is best advised to take the correspondence seriously and deal with it in such a manner as though the threatened action will be seen through to its conclusion.

When a solicitor takes instructions from a client, it is only when he or she is satisfied that the client has a valid claim that they would write a formal letter to the prospective defendant, setting out full details of the claim. This is called the

Letter of Claim. In cases of professional negligence, a preliminary notice would usually be sent prior to the Letter of Claim.

This notice would contain the following information:

- The identity of the claimant (client).
- A brief outline of the claimant's grievance against the professional.
- A general indication of the financial value of the potential claim.

This notice should be addressed to the therapist asking him or her to inform his professional indemnity insurers, if any, immediately. The therapist, or the therapist's solicitor, has 21 days to acknowledge receipt of this letter. Other than this acknowledgement, the preliminary notice places no obligation upon either party to take any further action (The Civil Procedure Rules, Professional Negligence Pre-action Protocol, Part B).

Following the preliminary notice, a Letter of Claim will be sent to the defendant. Whether or not you are disputing the claim, there is a requirement to acknowledge receipt of the letter within 21 days. The letter will normally be addressed to the therapist in person. However, if the solicitor is already aware that you have legal representation, then they will usually write directly to your solicitors. They will also enclose a copy for your insurers if you are likely to be insured against the claim.

The Letter of Claim will include the following information:

- Sufficient details to enable you to understand and investigate the claim without the need to seek extensive further information.
- Copies of any documents which the ex-client is relying on.
- Request for a prompt acknowledgement of the letter, followed by a written response within a reasonable period (generally one month).
- State where court proceedings will be issued if the full response is not submitted within the relevant time period.
- May identify and request disclosure of any essential documents in your possession, for example counselling notes.
- State whether or not the ex-client wishes to enter into any form of alternative dispute resolution.
- Draw your attention to the court's powers to impose sanctions for failure to comply with the directions.

If the therapist is disputing all or part of the claim, his or her letter of response would need to include the following information:

- Detailed reasons why the claim is not accepted, identifying which of the client's claims, if any, are accepted and which are disputed.
- Enclose copies of the essential documents on which the therapist relies.
- Enclose copies of documents asked for by the client, or explain why they are not enclosed.

- Identify and ask for disclosure of any essential documents in the client's possession.
- State whether the therapist is prepared to enter into any method of alternative dispute resolution.

In Scotland, although there is no formal preliminary notice or Letter of Claim, it is likely that the therapist will receive a solicitor's letter, setting out the basic details of the claim being made against the therapist and advising the therapist to inform his/her professional indemnity insurers. There is no requirement to acknowledge this letter. However, upon receipt of the letter, the therapist should seek legal advice, as legal proceedings are almost certainly going to be raised.

To make initial enquiries on your legal position, the following avenues are a good place to start:

- The Citizens Advice Bureau provides confidential legal advice.
- Contact the free Legal Help Line provided through your professional indemnity insurance company for advice.
- Contact the legal department of your professional association.

However, in responding to a Letter of Claim and observing certain time limits outlined above, it is clear that the therapist would need to consult a solicitor. The confidential services and help lines mentioned above may be useful for general enquiries but will not assist a therapist who requires expertise in a specialist area such as professional negligence. There are number of solicitors who have experience of handling such cases and the Law Society is a good place to start when searching for a suitable solicitor.

Solicitors letters are typically written in a formal and intimidating style. However, this is often deceptive. In deciding how to respond or even to do nothing, it is helpful to have some knowledge of the purpose of such letters and their role in the legal process. Knowledge weakens the intimidatory effect and enables the recipient to make considered and rational decisions in response the letter's contents. In some instances a solicitor's letter may be followed by the threat of court orders or the court order itself.

2 Court Orders

What are the aims of this area of law and its main applications?

Therapy is based on gaining and honouring the trust of clients and client confidentiality. For this reason, requests for disclosure of notes and any other information by courts are viewed by therapists as going against these fundamental principles. Historically, lawyers used disclosure in order to extract all potentially useful or interesting information, so that it became common for solicitors to embark on a fishing expedition to get hold of anything that may be adverse to the opponent's case (Jenkins et al., 2004: 81). However, this practice is now discouraged by the courts as being contrary to procedural fairness. Parties to civil proceedings are now restricted to obtaining evidence that is *relevant* to their dispute. This provides some protection for therapists' notes where the content is irrelevant to the case.

However, at the point of writing notes, therapists will usually find it difficult to anticipate what might be considered relevant to some future court case. Therefore, the prudent approach to writing notes is to bear in mind that all or part of the notes may be subject to court disclosure. Therapists may also be required to disclose emails, contracts and any other such documents that could be relevant to the case in question. The main objectives of the disclosure of these documents are to provide the parties in the case with sufficient information to enable them to resolve the dispute without the cost of taking it to court; and, in the event of a court case, to ensure that any decisions made by the courts are based on all the available relevant information. Examples of cases where such disclosures would arise are claims for injury arising from car accidents and claims for work-related injury.

There are two types of disclosure that therapists need to concern themselves with. The first is that of *pre-action disclosure* where an individual may be ordered by a court to provide documents to a prospective claimant to discover whether he/she has a viable case (Pattenden, 2003: 452). The second is that of *standard disclosure* under the Civil Procedure Rules 1998, which apply once court proceedings are underway. This chapter provides an outline of both types of disclosure.

Pre-action disclosure

What is pre-action disclosure?

An application for pre-action disclosure takes place *before court proceedings have started* and the purpose is to elicit any useful information that may be useful to a potential claim. Pre-action disclosure is governed by the Supreme Court Act 1981 and County Courts Act 1984. Under pre-action disclosure the court has the power to order a person who is not a party to the proceedings and who appears to the court to be likely to have in his or her possession, custody or power, any documents which are relevant to the issue arising out of the claim.

Therapists are obliged to disclose whether those documents are in their possession, custody or power and to produce such of those documents as are in their possession, custody or power to the applicant or on conditions, which are specified in the order:

- To the applicant's legal advisers; or
- To the applicant's legal advisers and any medical or other professional adviser of the applicant; or
- If the applicant has no legal adviser, to any medical or other professional adviser of the applicant (s34 (2). Supreme Court Act 1981).

The application must be supported by evidence and the court may make an order for disclosure only where:

- The respondent is likely to be a party to subsequent proceedings.
- The applicant is also likely to be a party to those proceedings.
- If proceedings have started, the documents will be disclosed under the standard procedure (discussed later).
- Disclosure before proceedings have started is desirable in order to (i) dispose fairly of the anticipated proceedings (ii) assist the dispute to be resolved without proceedings or (iii) save costs (Civil Procedure Rules 1998 r31.16).

What is the procedure for pre-action disclosure?

When producing documents for pre-action disclosure therapists would need to:

- Provide a list of documents in their possession.
- Allow a time and place for those documents to be inspected.
- Produce photocopies as required for the person who obtained the order, or to the court itself if ordered to do so.

Appropriate places to allow inspection of the documents are usually a solicitor's office or the usual place of custody of the documents, meaning the office where they are kept. However, in the case of therapist's counselling notes, it may not be appropriate to allow inspection in their home or office, so arrangements might need to be made for the inspection at another more neutral place, such as the court office itself.

If a therapist fails to comply with a pre-action disclosure order, the court can require any documents to be produced at a time and place of its choosing.

In what format should the documents be produced?

Any *documents produced for inspection* should be the originals and not photocopies. If ordered to produce counselling notes, they should be in the original form, whether handwritten, typed, taped or on computer disc or hard drive. It is not necessary to hand over the originals unless the court requires it, but *true* copies of those originals must be provided. Good quality photocopies of handwritten material and legible printouts of material held on computer will usually be sufficient to satisfy the requirements for true copies (Supreme Court Act order 24. 11A (1)). Once the documents are produced the court may deal with them in such manner as it thinks fit (Supreme Court Act 1981, order 24 rule 12).

The above rules in relation to pre-action disclosure do not apply in Scotland. However, the Administration of Justice (Scotland) Act 1972 makes provision, in certain circumstances, for the recovery of documents in advance of court proceedings being raised. It gives the court the power to order the inspection and preservation of documents and/or other property to which the court thinks a question might arise, not only in civil proceedings which have already been raised, but also in proceedings that are likely to be raised (s.1 Administration of Justice (Scotland) Act 1972). However, the court will usually only order recovery of documents in advance of proceedings being raised if there is a real risk that they will be lost or destroyed.

Standard Disclosure

What is standard disclosure under the civil procedure rules 1998?

- Standard disclosure takes place once proceedings have started. The purpose is to obtain as much relevant information as possible to strengthen your case.
- It is a procedural step whereby each party searches for and discloses to the other by a prescribed list, known as Form N265 (see example at the end of this chapter), the existence of certain documents, which are or have been in their control.
- Inspection is the process whereby the party receiving the N265 list has the right to look at the contents of documents where no privilege protecting documents from inspection is claimed. Privilege is covered later on in this chapter.

Therapists do not have to be a party to proceedings in a court of law to have an order for disclosure made against them. The meaning of disclosure is simple. A party discloses a document by stating that the document exists or has existed (Civil Procedure Rules rule 31.2 Section A). There is a standard procedure to follow for disclosure, which is discussed later.

What will the standard disclosure require therapists to disclose?

When giving standard disclosure, therapists are required to make a reasonable search and disclosure of documents, which adversely affects or supports another party's case. In deciding the reasonableness of a search for documents, therapists need to have regard to the nature and complexity of the proceedings in question and the significance to the case of any notes made during the counselling process. It is important for them to be aware that their duty to disclose counselling notes, for example, is limited to those notes, which are or have been in their control. In circumstances where the therapist is employed by, or is in the control of, an organisation or an employee assistance programme, for the purposes of disclosure, the counselling notes are owned or in the control of the organisation or programme. In comparison, where a therapist is in private practice, notes are considered to be in their physical possession or control for the purposes of standard disclosure.

Can therapists object to the production of documents?

A therapist may have serious concerns about disclosing information in an open courtroom. Typical concerns would be damaging an ongoing therapeutic relationship, harming the client's well-being or a concern about harming the client's case. In some instances therapists particularly of a psychoanalytical tradition have argued that any disclosure would be contrary to their professional ethics of protecting client confidentiality and privacy. In any of these circumstances, the therapist may consider that they have conscientious objections to disclosing any information to the court. The court holds the power to determine the validity of any of the objections. Any decision is likely to be based on a combination of the extent to which the court considers the objections to be well founded and the significance of the information in question to the court case. Thus any concerns therapists may have about the potential damage of disclosure to the therapeutic relationship, are weighed against the interests of achieving justice for all the parties concerned.

Therapists wishing to object to the production of any documentation in their possession must do so to the court immediately upon receipt of an order for disclosure. The court will decide whether the therapist must comply with that order. To assess the merits of the objections properly, the court is likely to inspect the documents before deciding whether to allow the objection. In these circumstances, the therapist must produce the documents to the court for private inspection (Supreme Court Act order 24 rule 13).

What is legal professional privilege and its relevance to disclosure?

Privilege permits certain individuals to ignore a lawful demand for information. Unlike an obligation of confidentiality, it operates exclusively as a shield (Pattenden, 2003: 452). Therapists are not privileged persons. Privileged persons include Sovereigns and their ambassadors, certain judicial persons and (in the case of partial privilege) justices of the peace (County Court Rules 1981 order 5 rule 2). Disclosure of documents also cannot be compelled if:

- Production is disproportionate to the issues in the case.
- The documents are privileged, protected by public interest immunity (PII) or a statute overriding the normal obligation to produce the documents.

Legal professional privilege can be claimed under one or more of the following heads:

- Letters and other communications passing between a client and his solicitor are privileged from inspection, provided they are written by or to the solicitor in his professional capacity and for the sole or dominant purpose of obtaining legal advice or assistance for the client. However, if part of a letter or communication does not relate to the giving of legal advice, that part of the letter will not be protected.
- Communications passing between the solicitor and a third party are privileged from production and inspection only if they come into existence after litigation is contemplated or commenced and they are made with a view to the litigation.
- Documents which have passed between the client and a third party are privileged if the main purpose for which they were produced was to obtain legal advice in respect of existing or contemplated litigation.

Communications between a party and his/her medical adviser, or his/her spiritual adviser or a non-professional friend or adviser, are not privileged although they maybe of the most confidential nature (Civil Procedure Rules section 31.3.19, section A). Confidentiality does not mean privilege. Therefore, therapists cannot use confidentiality of information in counselling notes as a reason to refuse disclosure if the document is not privileged, as information that has been communicated by one person to another in confidence is not, in itself, sufficient ground for protection from disclosure.

It follows, therefore, that when a court order is received requiring the disclosure of documents and notes held by therapists, they must comply with that order. Failure to do so will result in contempt of court, which could carry a fine or period of imprisonment for the therapist. Recent case law suggests that the more focused the complaint and more limited the disclosure sought, the easier it will be for a court to exercise its discretion in favour of pre-action disclosure, even where the complaint might seem somewhat speculative (*Rose v. Lynx Express Ltd and Bridgepoint*, 2004).

What is meant by a document?

A document is defined as anything in which information of any description is recorded (Civil Procedure Rules 1998, r 31.4). It is not restricted to paper records but extends to anything upon which information is recorded in a manner intelligible to the senses, or capable of being made intelligible by the use of equipment (Civil Procedure Rules 1998, r 31.4.1 section A). This in effect includes tape recordings of sessions or information stored on computers or disc, photographs, videos, CDs, minutes, contracts, emails and jottings on scraps of paper. Drawings and writing produced by the client as part of the therapy will also be regarded as documents for these purposes.

What is the standard procedure for disclosure?

When therapists receive a court order to disclose documents, they must disclose any and all documents in their possession relating to the case in question. After making a reasonable search for:

- Documents which a party is relying on, or
- Documents which adversely affect their own case, or another party's case, or
- Documents which support another party's case

the procedure for the standard disclosure should be followed in this way (Civil Procedure Rules 1998, r 31.10).

Each party must make and serve on every other party, a list of documents in the relevant practice form (Form N265). A copy of this is available at http://www.courtservice.gov.uk/cms/media/n265_eng.pdf and is also included at the end of this chapter. The form is divided into three parts:

PART 1 DOCUMENTS

This list must identify the documents in the therapist's control which they do not object to being inspected. This must be done in as convenient an order and manner as possible; for instance, by listing them in date order and numbering them consecutively. Examples of wording may be as follows: 'counselling notes dated between January and July 2005.'

PART 2 DOCUMENTS

This list must indicate those documents in respect of which the party claims a right or duty to withhold inspection, on the basis of privilege. Like Part 1 documents, these must be numbered. With regard to privilege, therapists need to give a general description and state clearly what their objections to disclosure are. An example of the wording that could be used in this case is mentioned below:

> [Nature of Document] 'Counselling notes relating to A N Offer'
> [Privilege Claimed] On the grounds/basis of ' they relate to issues which are not connected or related to this claim and could if disclosed, cause emotional harm to the client if read out in court, together with the information likely to be used by the other side in a detrimental and prejudicial manner.'

PART 3 DOCUMENTS

This section must list those documents which the therapist once had, but no longer has in his or her control. For each document listed, state when it was last in the therapist's control and where it is now.

Disclosure statement

A disclosure statement is a statement made by the party disclosing the documents. It sets out:

- The extent of the search that has been made to locate documents that the therapist is required to disclose.
- Certification that the practitioner understands the duty to disclose documents.
- Certification that to the best of their knowledge the therapist has carried out that duty.

The disclosure statement to be attached to a list of documents is as follows:

'I [*the person making the statement and why that person is the appropriate person to make it*], state that I have carried out a reasonable and proportionate search to locate all the documents which I am required to disclose under the order made by the court on———day of ——————————

I did not search
for documents predating _____
for documents located elsewhere than_____
for documents in categories other than_____

I certify that I understand the duty of disclosure and to the best of my knowledge I have carried out that duty. I certify that the list above is a complete list of all documents which are or have been in my control and which I am obliged under the said Order to disclose.'

It is crucial to ensure that all parts of the form are completed thoroughly and truthfully. For instance, if certain documents are omitted from the list in Part 1, which the other party expected to see or were aware of their existence, then an application for specific disclosure can be made. Part 3 should also be clear and accurate, as a party to the proceedings may want to trace and obtain a copy of a relevant document.

When disclosing any documents and where therapists are considering objecting to the production of documents they should consider their choices and reasons for objecting carefully. For example, if a party is dissatisfied with the disclosure provided by the therapist and believes it to be inadequate, then he or she can make an application for an order for specific disclosure (CPR 1998, r 31.12). In deciding whether to make an order for specific disclosure, the court will take into consideration all the circumstances of the case and if it concludes that you have failed to comply with the obligation, it will require you to disclose specific documents or classes of documents and also carry out a search as specified by the court order.

In Scotland, disclosure is in most cases sought by way of a procedure known as 'commission and diligence'. The party seeking to recover documents drafts a 'specification of documents', which sets out the type of document they seek to recover. These documents must be relevant to the case. If the party is able to satisfy the court that the documents are relevant, the court will grant an order that the documents must be produced by the person who has them in their custody. Accordingly, if a therapist's records are being sought, the therapist will receive a copy of the 'specification of documents', along with a copy of the court order ordering production. The therapist should then consider the terms of the 'specification of documents', to see whether he/she has any documents falling within its terms. If there is any doubt as to the meaning of the 'specification' or as to whether certain documents should be produced, therapists should seek legal advice. This is especially the case where the therapist wishes to try to claim confidentiality of any of the records. When producing documents, therapists will be required to produce all documents in their custody or possession. Originals should be produced, although photocopies are acceptable if it is necessary to hold on to the records themselves, for example, for the purpose of ongoing treatment. The documents should be returned to the solicitor of the party who is seeking disclosure of the documents, along with a form stating either that the therapist has no documents falling within the terms of the 'specification', or that the documents which are being produced are all the relevant documents in the hands of the therapist. If the therapist wishes to claim confidentiality in any document, the documents must still be produced, but in a sealed envelope or package. The issue as to whether or not the envelope should be opened, and the documents in question, will then be discussed before the court.

If the party seeking the documents is not satisfied that the therapist has produced all relevant documents, they can cite the therapist to appear at a hearing, called a 'commission'. This hearing is not presided over by a judge, but the therapist will be required to take an oath. The therapist can then be asked questions. For example whether they have, or ever had any other relevant documents and, if so, what happened to them.

Seeking advice

Therapists who receive an order to disclose documents under either of the aforementioned procedures and who are uncertain about anything they are being asked to do, should telephone the court that made the order, to seek clarification. It is important to do this as quickly as possible after receiving an order. Undue delay may suggest a lack of professionalism or imply disrespect towards the court and therefore increase the difficulty encountered if the therapist wishes to make any argument concerning restricting the disclosure of part or all of the records. In Scotland, if the therapist is uncertain about anything they have to do in response to the court order, they should seek legal advice.

Typically, orders are sought to obtain information that is relevant to a solicitor's client's case or to require the therapist to appear as a witness. The variety of court orders and their purposes are considered in the next chapter.

Standard Disclosure takes place in Form N265, which is shown below.

List of documents:
standard disclosure

Notes:

- The rules relating to standard disclosure are contained in Part 31 of the Civil Procedure Rules.
- Documents to be included under standard disclosure are contained in Rule 31.6
- A document has or will have been in your control if you have or have had possession, or a right of possession, of it or a right to inspect or take copies of it.

Disclosure Statement

I state that I have carried out a reasonable and proportionate search to locate all the documents which I am required to disclose under the order made by the court on (*insert date*)

(I did not search for documents –

1. pre-dating
2. located elsewhere than
3. in categories other than)

I certify that I understand the duty of disclosure and to the best of my knowledge I have carried out that duty. I further certify that the list of documents set out in or attached to this form, is a complete list of all documents which are or have been in my control and which I am obliged under the order to disclose.

I understand that I must inform the court and the other parties immediately if any further document required to be disclosed by Rule 31.6 comes into my control at any time before the conclusion of the case.

(I have not permitted inspection of documents within the category or class of documents (as set out below) required to be disclosed under Rule 31(6)(b)or (c) on the grounds that to do so would be disproportionate to the issues in the case.)

Signed		Date	

(Claimant)(Defendant)(litigation friend)

Position or office held (*if signing on behalf of firm or company*)
Please state why you are the appropriate person to make the disclosure statement.

```

```

I have control of the documents numbered and listed here. I do not object to you inspecting them/producing copies.

List and number here,
in a convenient order,
the documents (or
bundles of documents
if of the same nature,
e.g. invoices) in your
control, which you do
not object to being
inspected. Give a
short description of
each document or
bundle so that it can be
identified, and say if it
is kept elsewhere
i.e. with a bank or
solicitor

I have control of the documents numbered and listed here, but I object to you inspecting them:

List and number here,
as above, the
documents in your
control which you
object to being
inspected.
(Rule 31.19)

Say what your   I object to you inspecting these documents because:
objections are

I have had the documents numbered and listed below, but they are no longer in my control.

List and number here,
the documents you
once had in your
control, but which you
no longer have. For
each document listed,
say when it was last in
your control and where it is now.

Writing Reports

Therapists and report writing for the legal system

Writing reports has become an increasingly common way in which therapists find themselves entering the legal arena. A request for a report can come directly from a client, a solicitor, a coroner, the police, the courts, both civil and criminal, and/or the Criminal Injuries Compensation Authority (CICA). The primary objective in producing any report is to ensure that the court or the relevant body making the request has available to them all the necessary information required to make a decision in the interests of justice.

Preparing reports for the legal system involves significantly different approaches to writing and constructing accounts of events from those involved in producing therapeutic case studies for training and professional development. However, many of the literary skills developed in producing therapeutic case studies can be successfully transferred to writing court reports if the author takes account of the different audience.

This chapter introduces therapists to the different kinds of reports they might be asked to prepare in the course of their work and the usual conventions that apply in preparing them. One of the first matters to be clarified on being asked to write a report, is to establish what type of report is being requested. This is essential information in order to decide what is required and whether you consider yourself to be adequately competent and qualified to prepare the report and whether it is appropriate for you to do so.

General principles to consider when preparing reports

There are a number of useful principles that apply to writing all reports intended for use in legal proceedings. It is worth bearing in mind that the document will often be read by a busy and sometimes impatient person who is accustomed to listening and reading concise details of legally significant facts. In the context of a courtroom, a judge cherishes clarity and brevity in order to be able to focus on the relevant issues. Therefore, reports need be set out so that arguments can be logically drawn from them. The judge will be wary of flattery, incompleteness or anything with a hint of emotional manipulation. It is imperative that therapists stay focused on the purpose of the report and include only the information that is required to achieve that purpose. You should strive to remain as impartial as possible.

Words or phrases that have been so overused that they have lost their meaning need to be avoided. For example the phrase 'behavioural problem' can be used to describe everything from fidgeting to arson and, therefore, may convey very little to the reader. Therapists are trained to communicate with clients in gentle and supportive terms and often emphasise the positive, so that clients remain motivated to make any desired changes to their lives. This style of communication is not appropriate when writing a report for the court. It is advisable to stay factual, focused and to avoid glossing over problems.

The best way of checking clarity is to read the report out loud to yourself. Pay attention to grammar and be aware that while an electronic spell check is useful, it cannot be relied upon. Spell checkers merely highlight those letter clusters that cannot be recognised as words and may suggest inappropriate words or those that are similar to the intended word but carry a different meaning. Reading through the text out loud helps to identify what has actually been written but may not have been intended. Our ears detect things that our eyes or computer can miss. Aim to produce short, simple sentences that fully express a single idea.

Some examples of reports written by experienced report writers can be found later in this chapter.

What are the different types of report and in what context could I be asked to prepare one?

Witness statements

A statement taken by the police following an incident or where the solicitor interviews the witness to obtain the facts is called the *initial statement* (or a proof of evidence). This should be as comprehensive as possible, with the aim of helping the reader to understand the case. A more *formal statement* (known as the witness statement) containing only that evidence which the witness will give at the hearing, is prepared at a later stage by the solicitor handling the case. This statement is one which will be made available to all parties before the hearing.

The witness is asked to provide evidence relating to what happened in a particular instance; this is a formal account of the facts relating to the matter under investigation. They are a witness of fact and are asked to recall what they saw or heard but not to give opinions. In such cases therapists will be required to state the facts as they remember them or have recorded in their notes. A therapist may be required to make a statement to the effect that their client was present at a specified time and date for the purpose of counselling. For example, the employers of a particular client may want to check that he or she was attending counselling rather than taking unauthorised leave in a case relating to unfair dismissal. The same evidence could provide an alibi in a murder case:

Mary was present at 13 Thornhill Road on Tuesday 1 February 2005 at 10.00 am for the purpose of receiving therapy. Mary left at 10.50 am when the session ended.

In some cases, a brief written report may be all that is required but in more serious cases or where the evidence is contested, the therapist will be required to produce the original records or other material evidence, such as a receipt for payment, in order to corroborate the facts.

Where a request for a witness statement is received and the counselling relationship with that particular client has ended, the therapist is likely to be concerned about breaching client confidentiality. Therapists will have competing interests; maintaining the client's trust on the one hand, while acknowledging their own legal obligations on the other. Refusal to supply a witness statement may not always be appropriate and is dependent upon the circumstances and seriousness of the case. For example, in criminal cases where the allegation is one of murder, the information requested could rule out a possible suspect. Refusal to supply the details could result in the therapist being accused of the serious charge of obstructing a police investigation. It is advisable to assess the circumstances of the particular case carefully and, if considered appropriate, comply with the request. The therapist will also have an ethical duty to contact the client to inform him/her that a request for a witness statement has been received and to obtain his/her informed consent if disclosure has not already been made.

The following example is fairly typical of an initial statement that would be taken down by the police:

Witness Statement

(CJ Act 1967, s9; MC Act 1980, ss.5A(3) (a) and 5B; MC Rules 1981. R.70)

Statement of...**Marian Shepherd**

Age if under 18............................(if over 18 insert 'over 18') Occupation **Student Counsellor**....................

This statement (consisting of......1......page(s) each signed by me) is true to the best of my knowledge and belief and I make it knowing that, if it is tendered in evidence, I shall be liable to prosecution if I have wilfully stated anything in it which I know to be false, or do not believe to be true.

Signature.. Date...

I am employed as a student counsellor at Wessex University

I had spent the morning of 10 January 2005 seeing clients at the university. At approximately 12.40 pm I was walking through the reception area of the student services building in which I work, when I found a lady, whom I now know to be Susan Jones, who had been assaulted. She was lying on the floor and there was blood pouring out from her forehead and her eye. I saw a woman wearing a long brown coat, with short cropped hair and a baseball cap running away from the scene. I recognised her as Jane Green, whom I had seen for a counselling session 15 minutes prior to the incident.

Home address:

....Postcode: ....

Home telephone No: ....Mobile: ....

E-mail address (if applicable and witness wishes to be contacted by e-mail): ....

Contact point (if different from above):

Address...

Male/Female (delete as appropriate)   Date and place of birth..............................

State dates of witness non-availability...

Does the person making this statement have any special needs if required to attend court and give evidence? If 'Yes', please enter details.......................................

....

Does the person making this statement need additional support as a vulnerable or intimidated witness? If 'Yes', please enter details..

....

Does the person making this statement give their consent to it being disclosed for the purposes of civil proceedings (e.g. child care proceedings)?...............................

Signature of witness...

There a number of conditions that apply when preparing the initial statement. It should:

- Be signed by the therapist.
- Contain a declaration to the effect that it is true to the best of their knowledge and belief, and the statement is made with the knowledge that if it is used in evidence, he or she will be liable to prosecution if anything within the statement is false.

- A copy of the statement is to be made available by the therapist or their legal representative to each of the parties to the proceedings before the hearing at which the statement is put forward as evidence. The parties to the case, or their respective solicitors, can object to the statement being used as evidence in the relevant proceedings within seven days of the statement being submitted. (s.9 Criminal Justice Act 1967)

Even if the therapist does not prepare the statement themselves, he or she will be responsible for ensuring that it is accurate and that all the words contained in the statement are their own. There have been cases where solicitors and the police have put subtle pressure on a witness to include a certain spin on a statement. Equally, solicitors have been known to construct sophisticated legal arguments in these statements, which in effect represented their own arguments in the case (*Barclays Bank plc* v. *O'Brien*, 1994). The courts have made it implicit that the purpose of a witness statement is to make clear in your own words, what the relevant evidence is and it is not an opportunity for solicitors to put forward their own case. In all cases therapists need to resist any such pressure.

In Scotland, the police can ask you to provide a written statement in respect of a criminal matter, which you will be required to sign. In civil proceedings, formal witness statements are not used, as almost all the evidence of witnesses to fact is given orally in court and not in written form. You may, however, be asked by a solicitor to provide a statement called a 'precognition'. The purpose of a precognition is to set out for the solicitor what information you have about the case. The precognition is not a formal document and, consequently, will not be produced to the court, or to the other parties to the case. Occasionally, witnesses are asked to provide a signed, formal statement called an 'affidavit', which is witnessed by a notary public and may be produced to the court. However, these are seldom used.

Expert reports

The main difference between witness reports and expert reports is that experts not only report the facts known to them but also give opinions about possible interpretations of those facts. There is no fixed test to qualify as an author of an expert report. Anyone who has special expertise in an area can be considered as an expert. Expertise does not depend on qualifications alone, although frequently the expert will be highly qualified in his or her field (Browne and Catlow, 2004: 33). The authors of such reports are usually at the top of their particular profession and any fact or opinion that is presented by the expert requires it to be based on a wealth of experience and knowledge on the particular area he or she professes to be an expert in.

The expert's overriding duty is to the court:

- They report on matters that are not within the common knowledge of the court.
- Assist in the task of resolving a dispute or examining a situation.
- Ensure the court has access to specialist information from an impartial and independent source.

Any request to write an expert witness report needs to be considered carefully in order to assess whether the therapist is competent and suitable to write it. The independent nature of the expert witness is an important characteristic as there have been cases where clients have asked their own therapists to write an 'expert report' for use in court. In these circumstances, therapists would need to make the following clear to their clients:

- A report put to the court by an independent expert who has never treated the client, will normally carry more weight than an 'expert' report put forward by the treating therapist, especially if the purpose of the report is to provide an assessment.
- In some circumstances, an expert report from a treating therapist may be requested, especially for proceedings concerning children and families where it is considered that increasing the number of professionals involved with the family would be disruptive to the best interests of the children.
- Clients need to know that the expert's responsibility is to the court and that they have responsibility to report all relevant facts, whether or not they are advantageous to the client.

If a therapist decides that they have the expertise and experience to produce an expert report on a client they have treated or on someone else's client, they should be aware that this is not something to be undertaken lightly. It is increasingly commonplace for expert witnesses to have received specific training in report writing and giving evidence in court, and perhaps to have shadowed other expert witnesses before taking on a case alone. People who offer their services as independent witnesses are normally expected to have adequate training. Treating therapists may have less opportunity for training, for their role prior to a case. Nonetheless, they should seek as much guidance as possible on how to undertake this work. In some circumstances they may prefer to be called as a witness of fact rather than as an expert. This is a less onerous role because the witness is not required to offer professional opinions and to be cross-examined on these. However, being a witness of fact about a client who has received therapy can be problematic and has it own challenges (see Chapters 6 and 7).

Responding to a request from a solicitor to write an expert report

A detailed explanation of how to respond to a solicitor's letter can be found in the section on solicitors' letters in Chapter 1. The solicitor will usually send out a letter of instruction setting out the context in which your opinion and experience is required. You are also responsible for making clear the limits of your expertise. Bearing in mind that the report is prepared with the knowledge that a trial at court could be the eventual outcome, you may be required to attend and give oral evidence, upon which you may be cross-examined.

A therapist who decides to accept the role of writing an expert report, would need to establish the intended purpose and reason for the request and address the more practical aspects, such as any fee payable. It is best practice to agree the terms and conditions with the solicitor before writing commences. A contract for writing the report would normally be made between the solicitor and the therapist, not the solicitor's client and the therapist. The court lays down a table of experts' fees and a rough guideline is also presented in the Chapter 5 on Payment of Expenses and Fees. In Scotland, the fees to be paid for the preparation of the report and any attendance at court is a matter to be decided between the expert therapist and the person instructing them.

Requesting all the information from the solicitor, which may assist in the preparation of the report, is a priority. Therapists need to obtain the following:

- Details of what is required: whether you are required to compile a preliminary or final report, attend meetings with solicitors and barristers/advocates and attend court, should alternative forms of settlement prove impossible.
- Details of the case.
- Your obligations as a therapist: for example, using reasonable skill and care in carrying out the instructions and preserving the confidentiality of information, documents and correspondence involved in the case.
- Fees, based on the amount of time, degree of skill and responsibility that is involved.
- Time limits: the date the report will need to be completed by, and the date of the final court hearing.

Requests for background information would need to include a request to be updated on all significant developments in the case. Failure to do this may result in the report not addressing an important aspect of the case, thereby reducing or negating its usefulness as a piece of evidence. In order to satisfy yourself that you are fully equipped with all the information and details necessary, it is a matter of good practice to send a letter to the solicitor confirming, as you understand it, the details/information upon which you are required to report. This will ensure that you have clearly understood what is required of you.

When these preliminary steps have been followed and the therapist is satisfied with the information supplied, the task of preparing the report may begin.

Establishing for which court the expert report is required

As different rules govern the Criminal and Civil Courts, and since in England the Family Court issues its own guidelines regarding the presentation of evidence where children and their families are concerned, therapists need to establish which court they are writing the report for.

Reports for civil proceedings

Writers of expert reports are under a duty to assist the court on matters within their area of expertise. The English courts have extensive powers to restrict expert evidence under Civil Procedure Rule 35.4:

- No party may call an expert, or put in evidence an expert report without the court's permission.
- When a party applies for permission under this rule, he must identify (a) the field of expertise on which he wishes to rely on expert evidence; and (b) where practicable the expert in that field, on whose evidence he wishes to rely.

In Scotland, the court's permission is not required to call an expert witness or lodge their report. However, given the costs involved in instructing expert witnesses, parties to proceedings will seldom use an expert unless their opinion is important and relevant to the case.

The vast majority of civil cases are resolved outside the courtroom, usually before the date set for the hearing. In England, this will usually be achieved through Alternative Dispute Resolution (ADR), which takes several forms. Even if ADR is not used it is more efficient and easier for those involved if the acting solicitors can encourage the parties to resolve the dispute by an out of court settlement. The production of a well-written and unbiased report can greatly assist in these circumstances and may prevent cases becoming long and pro-tracted and being trawled through the courts in ways that may not be beneficial to the parties concerned.

In civil proceedings, if the party who requested the report decides not to use the expert therapist's report in their case, the report will be protected by litigation privi-lege. This means that the report will not be disclosed in court. The experts in the case cannot themselves claim this privilege; privilege can only be invoked by the party who requested the report. However, reports relating to children's cases and those for the prosecution during a criminal investigation have to be disclosed regardless of whether or not the party requesting the report is intending to rely on it.

Reports for criminal proceedings

In criminal cases the responsibilities of the person writing the report are similar to those in civil proceedings, with the exception that the general rule is for oral evidence to be given by the author and the quality of that evidence to be tested in cross-examination. An expert report is allowed as evidence in criminal proceed-ings, regardless of whether or not the person making it attends the hearing to give oral evidence. In the unusual circumstances where the reporting expert therapist will not be giving oral evidence, the report can only be used as evidence with the permission of the court. Therapists providing expert witness reports should expect to give oral evidence unless the court directs them otherwise. When deciding upon this issue the court will take the following factors into consideration:

- The content of the report.
- Reasons why oral evidence is not being given.
- The likely benefit or detriment of providing oral evidence.
- Any other circumstances that the court believes to be relevant.

Accordingly, unless all parties accept the report in its entirety and the court decides to grant leave, therapists would normally be expected to give oral evidence when involved in criminal proceedings.

Reports for children's proceedings

The following three factors underpin the approach of the Family Courts to children's cases and evidence in general:

1   At present it is a contempt of court to publish information relating to proceedings brought under the Children Act (s.12 Administration of Justice Act 1960) and makes it a criminal offence for any person to publish any material that would identify, or is likely to identify, a child as being involved in Family Court proceedings, unless the court decides that the welfare of the child requires disclosure (s. 97(2) of the Children Act 1989). However, section 62 of the Children Act 2004 (not yet commenced) is set to change the law relating to disclosure of information in family proceedings cases involving children. The key changes do two things: (1) limit the potential criminal offence concerning the communication (technically referred to as publication) of information from family proceedings to the public or any section of the public and (2) clarifying that it would not be a potential contempt to communicate information that is authorised by the Rules of Court. The law relating to disclosure in children's cases provides for the sharing of information between those with a legitimate need for that information. For example, professionals involved in such cases may require disclosure of information, i.e. experts may want to consult with child protection professionals for the purpose of preparing a report that takes into consideration all relevant factors in the case. (Department for Constitutional Affairs, 2005)
2   Proceedings are non-adversarial, unlike the usual proceedings in civil and criminal courts, as they are conducted with the overriding objective of reaching decisions that are in the best interests of the child. The court does not concern itself with whether or not the decision is particularly favourable to one party or the other.
3   The court has a duty imposed upon it to avoid delay and to be proactive in timetabling cases. (s.1 (2) Children Act 1989)

Commonly, therapists are instructed by the solicitor or court to provide a report for the Family Court, relating to the suitability of a child for therapy, the effect on a child of reduced or increased contact with an absent parent and the effect on a child of being placed in therapy (Pollecoff, 2002: 64). For cases which relate to access by parent(s) and child care proceedings, a welfare checklist is commonly used by experts when presenting their written evidence. The expert witness is required to address and report on:

- The ascertainable wishes and feelings of the child.
- The child's physical, emotional and educational needs.
- The likely effect on the child of any change in circumstances.
- The child's age, gender, background and any characteristics which the court considers relevant.
- Any harm the child has suffered or is at risk of suffering.

- How capable each of the parents is, and any other person in relation to whom the court considers the question to be relevant, in meeting the child's needs.
- The range of powers available to the court in the proceedings in question. (s.1 (3) Children Act 1989)

Because confidentiality plays an important role in children's cases, the courts play a much more proactive role in deciding what expert evidence is to be called. The court is concerned with making a decision that is in the child's best interests. Therefore, the welfare list is structured so that the therapist will be able to present the facts and an opinion, in view of identifying risks and the needs of the child in question. The duty to be objective and not to mislead is vital as the child's welfare is at stake, and his/her interests are paramount. An absence of objectivity may result in a child being wrongly placed with the possibility of them being put at risk unnecessarily. A misleading opinion may well inhibit a proper assessment of a particular case by the non-medical professional advisers and may also lead parties, and in particular parents, to false views and hopes (*Re J* 1991).

The concept of litigation privilege which exists in other proceedings does not apply to reports in children's proceedings. For instance, a party who obtains permission from the court to commission a report from an expert therapist, and discovers that the report is in fact detrimental to their case, cannot then go on to refuse to disclose that report to the other parties and to the court. Thus, whatever opinion the therapist has come to, it will be read by the judge, even if it is contrary to the interests of the instructing party. For example, in the 1996 case of *Re L* (*a minor*) (*police investigation*), heroin addict parents obtained the leave of the court to show the papers to a consultant chemical pathologist with a view to demonstrating that their two-year-old could have ingested a substantial quantity of methadone accidentally. The report was adverse, as it disproved their argument, but had to be disclosed.

Proceedings relating to children in Scotland are governed by the Children (Scotland) Act 1995; there are no dedicated Family Courts in Scotland. Some family cases, for example those dealing with custody of children following separation and or divorce, are dealt within the courts. In such instances, the normal rules relating to the writing and use of expert reports in court proceedings will apply. As an alternative to court proceedings, where a child under the age of 16 has committed an offence or is otherwise in need of care or protection, this will usually be dealt with by the Children's Hearing system. This is much less formal than a court process and is designed to be more accessible for the child and their family. The hearing is usually presided over by a Children's Panel, comprising three lay people. The decision as to whether or not to refer a child to a Children's Panel is taken by a Reporter. A therapist can be invited to provide a report for the Reporter or a Children's Hearing in relation to issues relevant to the welfare of the child. Any report provided will be confidential and will only be disclosed to the parties involved in the hearing.

The structure of an expert report

Addressing the report to the court, rather than to the instructing party, is a matter of necessity; the duty to a court overrides any obligation and duty to the instructing party. When writing the report it is important to be mindful that the report could be used in evidence and care should be taken to make it inclusive of all relevant facts. A report of this nature must comply with the following:

- It should be addressed to the court and not to the party from whom you have received your instructions.
- Set out your qualifications and sometimes your experience that qualifies you to be an expert.
- State your sources of information, documentary and in person, typically by interviewing the person concerned.
- Contain a section which sets out the substance of all the facts known to you that are relevant to the case. It is important to be attentive to distinguishing fact from opinion in all expert reports but especially when the report is from a treating therapist. Facts are determined by objective standards and processes. This will usually exclude the subjective experience of the therapist.
- Distinguish facts that are known directly to you from facts that are reported to you and state the sources of the latter.
- Give your professional opinion based on the facts and on reasoned analysis.
- Where a fact could support several opinions, state all of these possible opinions and give reasoned argument in favour of any preferred opinion (sometimes it is not possible to choose a single opinion). Indicating the types of facts required to resolve a choice between possible opinions may help the court carry out its task and to obtain the missing information.
- Give details of any literature or other material which you have relied upon in making the report – see the psychologist's report later in this chapter as an example of how to do this.
- Provide a summary of the conclusions reached.
- Include a statement of truth confirming that you understand that your duty is to the court, and that you have complied with that duty.

A full version of a statement of truth for civil proceedings in England and Wales follows:

I understand that in preparing this report my duty is to the court and I consider that I have complied with that duty. I believe that the facts that I have stated are true and that the opinions I have expressed are correct.

a. I understand my primary duty in written reports and giving evidence is to the court, rather than the party who instructed me.
b. I have endeavoured in my report and in my opinions to be accurate and have covered all relevant issues concerning the matters stated which I have been asked to address.
c. I have endeavoured to include in my report those matters which I have knowledge of, or of which I have been made aware, that might adversely affect the validity of my opinion.

d.   I have indicated the sources of all information I have used.
e.   I have not without forming an independent view included or excluded anything which has been suggested to me by others (in particular the instructing party).
f.   I will notify those instructing me immediately, and confirm it in writing, if for any reason my existing report requires any correction or qualification.
g.   I understand that:

   (i)   My report, subject to any corrections before swearing as to its correctness, will form the evidence to be given under oath or affirmation;
   (ii) I may be cross-examined on my report by a cross-examiner assisted by an expert;
   (iii) I am likely to be the subject of public adverse criticism by the judge if the court concludes that I have not taken reasonable care in trying to meet the standards set out above;
   (iv) I confirm that I have not entered into any agreement where the amount or payment of the fee is in any way dependent on the outcome of the case.

In practice, this statement of truth is often given in shorter version, as in the examples in the next section. However, the full version provides a useful summary of the legal responsibilities of an expert witness.

Examples of expert witness reports

Two types of expert report are offered as examples. Both reports have been written by experienced report writers around fictional cases. The first is by a treating therapist, in this case a school counsellor concerning a child where an English local authority is seeking a care order in the family court. The second case is typical of independent assessments undertaken by clinical psychologists of the psychological impact of a traumatic event, in this case a road traffic accident.

In each case the expert has taken into consideration that they have been appointed to write the report as someone with knowledge or experience of a particular field or discipline beyond that expected of a lay person. This presents a challenge for any expert because the definition presumes that the expert will strive to make specialist knowledge and practice readily comprehensible to the non-expert. This requires a different type of writing from communication between professionals who share a common training and language. Everyday language and explanations are to be preferred over professional jargon and shorthand. The other major challenge is meeting the expectations of a legal readership. In legal proceedings, it is usual practice to be attentive to distinguishing fact and opinion, however expert that opinion. Facts are typically things that have been directly observed such as someone's behaviour or what someone says. For example, a young person is routinely ten minutes late for an appointment (fact). She explains that she has to take a younger member of her family to be cared for by a relative on the way to the appointment. She has to wait for the relative to return from work and leaves by the first available bus to travel to the appointment. She regrets the lateness (that she said these words is fact, if she did offer them as an explanation). However, it is opinion as to whether the lateness represents commendable social responsibility towards a younger member of her family or is evidence of a reluctance to participate in the appointment. Further facts would be required to secure an opinion, perhaps concerning the availability of other means of transport and the quality of her participation at the appointment. When checking whether an opinion is fully justified, lawyers like to be able to distinguish the facts that form the basis of the opinion from the opinion itself, even if it is an expert professional opinion.

The circumstances in which expert reports are requested can be very varied, resulting in quite different instructions to the report writer. Experienced report writers are better placed to identify variations in instructions. An inexperienced report writer may find it useful to ask whether there is anything unusual in the instructions and to establish the background to the instructions being issued. In the first example, a letter of instruction is provided.

Letter of instruction to expert witness, the treating therapist, for the Family Court

Dear Mrs Kirkby

Re. Katy Walker
Date of Birth: 27.7.93

I write further to our recent telephone conversation of [date]. Thank you for agreeing to provide a report to the court in relation to Katy Walker. Please note that this is a joint instruction and details of those instructing you can be found below.

The representatives

In this case;

1. I represent Katy Walker, the child in these proceedings on the instructions of the children's guardian, … of the Children and Family Court Advisory Support Service (CAFCASS), [*address and telephone number provided*]
2. The child's mother Mary McDonald is represented by … at [*name and address of solicitor's firm*]
3. The child's father is represented by … at …
4. The Applicant Local Authority Wessex County Council is represented by … of …
5. The social worker dealing with the case is … who is based at …

The nature of the instructions

You are being instructed jointly by this firm and by the local authority only, but on the basis that you will provide an independent expert opinion entirely independent of us both.

You have been given permission by the court, to meet with Katy. This permission is necessary because you are, for these purposes meeting with her as an expert witness in the course of care proceedings, not in your clinical role. How you meet with Katy is of course a matter for your own individual discretion. Further, the parties wish me to say that you should not construe these instructions as implying that you should raise with Katy or discuss with her matters which you do not consider to be in her best interests.

You are also of course at liberty to discuss the case with any other expert instructed in this case if you feel that would assist you in writing your report. It is, however, essential both to your role as an independent expert and to the parties' perception of your independent status, that if you do have informal discussions or correspondence with any of the professionals or the lay parties involved in the case, you should make a note of all such discussions. You should also disclose the fact that you have had them when you write your report, and explain what influence, if any, such discussions have had upon your thinking and your conclusions.

If you need further information, please contact me. I will provide it after consultation with the other legal advisers involved. If documents are exchanged with one party, please copy them to all the others. Where possible, communication is best achieved by fax or by letter.

The background

I enclose photocopies of those documents that it has been agreed are necessary for you to consider. (Please see schedule attached.) If, having perused the documents enclosed you consider that you require any further documents, please contact me and I will consult with the other legal advisors.

Wessex County Council has made an application for a care order in respect of Katy at Wessex Family Proceedings Court and Katy is a respondent to this application. You are familiar with the background to this case.

Your instructions

You are requested kindly to consider the papers and provide your opinion on the following issues:

1. Please provide a history of your involvement with Katy and the areas covered during the time that you have seen her.
2. What is the nature and quality of Katy's attachment to her mother?
3. In your opinion are there any issues that have arisen which would impact on contact between Katy and her mother including unsupervised contact.
4. Are there any issues that you wish to comment on at this stage concerning Katy's welfare?

In giving your opinion, please have regard always to the principle that in determining any question with respect to the children, the child's welfare is the court's paramount consideration. If during the course of your investigation, other issues appear to you to become relevant, please immediately contact me. I will consult with the other legal advisors and will consider whether the scope of your instructions should be amended.

Factual issues

Unless you have been specifically asked to do so you should avoid expressing a view regarding the factual disputes as this, of course, is the province of the court at the final hearing. Where appropriate it will be of assistance if you are able to express your opinion on the basis of alternative findings regarding the factual dispute(s).

Disclosure

We are under a duty to disclose the report to the court and the other parties and we will circulate your report on receipt. If you believe that as a rare exception to the general rule it should not be disclosed to any party please let us know and we shall seek the court's directions.

Wording of the report

In order to comply with court rules I should be grateful if you would include in your report the following:

1. Details of your qualifications.
2. Details of any literature or other materials that you rely on should be referred to and enclosed.
3. A summary should be provided of your conclusions.
4. A confirmation statement, such as:

   'I understand that it is my duty as an expert to help the court on matters within my expertise and that this duty overrides any obligation that I may have to the solicitors or their client from whom I have received instructions.'

5. The report should contain a statement setting out the substance of the instructions; this should summarise the facts and instructions given to the expert that are material to the opinions/valuation expressed in the report.
6. Conclude your report, above your signature, with a statement as follows:

   'I believe that the facts I have stated in this report are true and that the opinions I have expressed are correct.'

The timetable pursuant to the above court order

Under the terms of the order your report is to be filed and served on … [date]. The report will need to reach me a little earlier than that (in order that, by that time and date,) so that copies of your report can be sent by me to the court office and the other solicitors by that time and date. It is crucial that you comply with this time limit as a subsequent timetable for the filing of statements and reports, and the final hearing, are dependent upon the receipt of your report by the due date. Could you also please note that the final hearing is listed for [date]. It is expected that you will please attend on the morning of ... [date]. If any of these dates and times are or become inconvenient to you, would you please let me know immediately, as an application may have to be made to vary the dates.

Funding

Because some of the parties to the proceedings have the benefit of Community Legal Services Funding certificate, a note of your hourly rate and the anticipated total costs of your report are needed as soon as possible, please, in order that the authority to meet your charges can be obtained in advance from the Legal Services Commission for you to undertake a report to an agreed financial limit at an agreed maximum hourly rate. If having set a limit you find this limit insufficient please let us know immediately and the parties will apply to the Legal Services Commission for further authority. On receipt of your invoice, application will be made to the Commission for funds to meet your account to the authorised limit. We should make it clear, however, that we shall not be able to pay any cheques over the authorised limit unless those changes are approved on assessment at the conclusion of the proceedings.

Many thanks in anticipation of your assistance.

Yours sincerely

The letter of instruction provides you with essential information; some of this is directly communicated. For example, the court hearing is concerned with care proceedings, in which the local authority could be granted responsibility for providing the care for a child rather than a case arising from a dispute between the parents about who will have primary responsibility for caring for the children or any of the other types of cases heard in family proceedings. Some of the important information may be less obvious. It is relatively rare for a Family Court to ask for a report from a therapist providing counselling to a child because they are reluctant to disturb ongoing therapeutic relationships. If a fully independent assessment is required an independent child psychologist or child psychiatrist would normally be instructed. If the child is seeing the relevant Child and Adolescent Mental Health Service or comparable service then they may be asked to provide a report. However, the request has been made to the current counsellor and it would be reasonable to ask the reason for this. It may be that there is a concern not to introduce additional professionals into the young person's life or there may be other reasons particular to that case. Usually the instructions would be issued by all the parties but in this case the parents have not been included, perhaps because they want to keep some distance from the therapeutic work, but again knowing the reasons for this variation from usual practice might be helpful information. Some of these issues may have been discussed prior to the issuing of the instructions in the preliminary telephone conversation. In this case the counsellor has agreed to provide the report but she could equally have refused the request, especially if she considered that her involvement in writing the report would disrupt the therapeutic relationship or be counterproductive for the child or young person. Typically counsellors are concerned only to provide reports in these circumstances with their client's consent.

The section that sets out the issues to be addressed in the report, in this case 'Your instructions', requires careful scrutiny as these should be restricted to your areas of expertise. If you are asked something outside your expertise, you make this clear within your report and you would not be expected to respond to that request. The report written in response to these instructions provides an example of a refusal to provide additional comments in section 4 as being outside the counsellor's area of expertise concerning the quality of the client's attachment to her mother.

Court Report concerning

**Katy Walker
DOB 27.07.93**

1. Background

I, Susanna Kirkby, am a school counsellor working in Wessex County Secondary School two days a week. I have been an accredited counsellor with the British Association for Counsellors and Psychotherapists (BACP) since 2001. I hold a postgraduate diploma in Counselling, which I obtained in 1997 from London University. I have also done further short courses on working with children and young people, bereavement and relationships. Prior to training as a counsellor I qualified and worked as a Registered General Nurse. I have been working at Wessex Secondary School since 1999 and also work in private practice with adults and young people.

As a school counsellor I am responsible for providing counselling two days a week. I counsel children for 50-minute sessions weekly or fortnightly. The children present with a variety of emotional, psychological, behavioural and mental health difficulties. Although primarily I work one-to-one with children I also occasionally do some work with children together with their parents, especially the younger children, but only if this feels appropriate for the child.

2. Instructions

This report was requested by David Oriel, solicitor for Katy within Care Proceedings on behalf of Katy and Wessex County Council pursuant to an order of the Wessex Family Proceedings Court dated the

In my letter of instruction [dated] I was requested to consider the papers provided and provide my opinion on the following issues:

1. Please provide a history of your involvement with Katy and the areas covered during the time that you have seen her.
2. What is the nature and quality of Katy's attachment to her mother?
3. In your opinion are there any issues that have arisen which would impact on contact between Katy and her mother including unsupervised contact?
4. Are there any other issues concerning Katy's welfare that you wish to comment on at this stage (concerning Katy's welfare)?

I will respond to each of these questions in order.

3. A history of my involvement with Katy and the areas covered during the time that I have seen her

I first started seeing Katy in September 2004, shortly after she had started at Wessex Secondary School. Katy's mother, Mary McDonald, asked that Katy have counselling and attended the first meeting at Katy's request. Since then I have seen Katy on a one-to-one basis. For the most part I have seen her weekly within school term time and we continue with ongoing counselling.

I have spoken to Katy about providing a report to the court concerning her counselling. She understands what is being requested and has given her consent to me preparing this report.

At our initial session Katy's mother, Mary McDonald, explained to me that she had had a problem with alcohol which was now under control and for which she was receiving support. She was concerned at the difficulty that Katy had in relating to her and both she and Katy seemed to think that this was a problem to do with Katy as Katy often got very angry.

The areas that we have covered during our sessions have been: triggers for Katy's anger, her relationships within her family, her relationships with peers and her self-esteem.

Katy has spoken of how much she misses her brother Andrew living with her, following his placement with foster parents in July last year, and how much she enjoys seeing him. Her relationship with her father seems important to her despite the fact that she does not see him very often. Her relationship with her mother is the most important relationship to Katy. She did not mention any violence from her mother until after she had been placed in foster care. She is clear that this has only happened when her mother is drunk and that otherwise Katy describes her as a very good mother.

Although Katy wants to return home she is anxious about her mother starting to drink again.

Katy is happy in school and has made some friends.

4. What is the nature and quality of Katy's attachment to her mother?

I have only seen Katy and her mother together once and therefore I can only comment on what Katy has said. Katy appears to be very attached to her mother and this is an important relationship to her. Katy has expressed the importance to her of seeing her mother as soon as possible as she has not been able to see her since she went into foster care. This would serve the purpose of reassuring Katy that her mother was alright.

I am not qualified to comment further on this.

5. Any issues, which have arisen that would impact on contact between Katy and her mother

As I have said above Katy would like some contact with her mother as soon as possible. However, Katy has not been able to confirm whether she would be able to tell someone if her mother was to cause her more violence.

6. Summary

In summary Katy has been able to form a therapeutic relationship with me which appears to be helpful to her. It is my intention to continue term-time weekly sessions for the time being.

She has close and important relationships within her family, which she wants to be maintained. She wants her mother to get better so that she can return home. She is, however, anxious about her mother continuing to drink.

I understand that it is my duty as an expert to help the court on matters within my expertise and that this duty overrides any obligation that I may have to the solicitors or their client from whom I have received instructions.

I believe that the facts I have stated in this report are true and that the opinions I have expressed are correct.

Signed ....

   Susannah Kirkby

Dated this day of 2005.

This is a very full report for one prepared by a counsellor who is involved in counselling the subject of the report, in part because the author has accepted instructions to provide information about the quality of the relationships within the family. If the report had been restricted to an account of the therapy undertaken, it might merely have been a statement of quantity of therapy provided over what duration and a brief factual summary of the main issues raised in the counselling. Typically, a full assessment of the relationships within a family would only be undertaken by an independent assessment by someone who has no connection with any ongoing therapy.

It is important to note that there are other ways in which counsellors can be drawn in to providing some input into court reports particularly in children's cases. If a child has disclosed a child protection issue then they may be asked to write a statement. When a child is in care, then Social Services are bound to hold reviews at a minimum of every six months. They may ask the school counsellor to contribute to a report by completing a standard form. If they are carrying out a formal assessment of the child's needs then they may again ask the counsellor to respond to a standard form. These contributions may end up as a part of the court report that is submitted to the court by the Local Authority. It is therefore always important that clients consent to any written report. Written reports may well be shown to clients by Social Services so that must always be kept in mind. Counsellors working with adult clients who have cases before the Family Court may also be asked to provide reports to the court about their work with the adult concerned. For example, in cases arising from the divorce of parents concerning the care and access arrangements for the children, the counsellor may be asked to provide a report of their work around issues such as anger, so that the court is informed whether such issues are being addressed by the client and about the client's motivation to function constructively within the restructured family relationships.

The second example illustrates another common source of requests for reports from expert witnesses with a therapeutic background. Compensation claims following an accident on the roads or at work are commonplace occurrences in civil proceedings. The amount of the compensation to a victim will usually be determined according to the degree of physical and psychological injury suffered. The level of compensation depends on determining the extent to which that trauma was additional to any underlying condition and likelihood of effective treatment. These involve technical diagnostic assessments which are most suited to clinical psychologists, who are the usual source of these reports.

Psychological Report

Re: James Alfred Atkinson

Prepared by: Dr. C. S. Rydal B.A., D.Clin. Psych., C.Psychol., A.F.B.Ps.S.
                 Consultant Clinical Psychologist

Qualifications: B.A. Honours in Psychology, University of Wessex
1976, D.Clin. Psych., University of Avon 1980

Registration: Chartered Clinical Psychologist, British Psychological Society

Positions held: Director of Clinical Psychology and Consultant
Clinical Psychologist, Wessex NHS Trust

**Date of
Interviews:**   12 October 2004

Location: The Wessex Independent Hospital

**Report
Requested by:**   Doctors Services Ltd

Instructions received:

This instruction has been made by Griffin Spencer and Smith in accordance with the 'Pre-Action Personal Injury Protocol' and the new 'Court Rules'.

A full examination of the claimant is required and your full written report shall deal with any relevant pre-accident history, the injuries sustained, treatment received and the present condition, dealing in particular with the capacity for work and giving a definitive prognosis.

Re: James Atkinson

I interviewed the above on 12 October 2004 for the purposes of preparing this report on the psychological aspects of the road traffic accident in which he was involved and which took place on 12 February 2004. The Beck Depression Inventory and the Impact of Event Scale were also administered.

I have read copies of the GP Medical Record covering the period 11 October 1988 to 4 August 2004, including a report of the counselling prepared by the practice counsellor, and the Accident and Emergency report from the Wessex General Hospital for 12 February 2004.

Background and progress to the time of assessment

The accident occurred on a Thursday evening at 8.42 pm. He was driving a heavy goods vehicle in the course of his work and was travelling on the Avon Dual Carriageway at Axminster when an Austin Healey sports car, crossing the dual carriageway, was in collision with his vehicle. He was thrown across the cab and said that he banged his shoulder and head on the passenger door. He remained conscious and his immediate concern was to bring his vehicle to a halt. He reported that he then climbed out of his vehicle to go to assist the occupants of the sports car but saw that the car was a 'crumpled mess' and he resisted looking inside the car for fear of what he might see. He said that he then 'froze' and did not know what to do. He had to be assisted by others at the scene who took control and sat him down at the road side.

The police and ambulance services attended and he recalled being 'out of it' at the scene. He recalled people trying to talk to him and that he was unable to respond. He was informed by the ambulance crew that 'nothing could be done' for the occupants of the car and this made him very distressed. He was taken by ambulance to the Accident and Emergency department of the W.G.H. where he was assessed and found to have no significant physical injuries. He reported, however, that at the hospital he was 'distressed and crying' and kept saying 'I've killed two people'. A nurse had to counsel him for between 30 and 45 minutes and reassure him that it had not been his fault and he was advised to seek counselling through his GP. He was also interviewed by the police in the hospital but was too distressed to give a statement. He was finally taken by the police back to his home at about 1.45 am.

At the time of the accident he was at the beginning of a night shift and, though he attempted to sleep on the night of the accident, he obtained little if any sleep. He stated that the accident kept going through his mind and that when the early morning news came on he saw the scene of the accident and the report that a recently engaged couple aged 27 and 24 had been killed. He was greatly distressed by this news and again later in the morning when he learned that the driver was the woman.

He reported that on the Friday his wife stayed at home with him and that he cried frequently throughout day. He stated that he was constantly preoccupied with thoughts and flashbacks of the accident and became more intensely upset each time the accident was reported on the news. His GP visited him at home and it is noted in the record that he was 'anxious and upset'. He did not go to work that evening, was given a sicknote by his GP and in the event did not return to work for a month. He said that on the Friday night he only obtained 2 or 3 hours of fitful sleep and was repeatedly disturbed by recalling the accident with frequent flashbacks of the point of impact and his first sight of the wrecked car.

He reported that his wife drove him into work on Saturday to complete the insurance forms. He noted that he felt very uneasy and jumpy on the journey. He said that when he arrived at work and saw his colleagues he burst into tears and had to be consoled by them. The owner of the transport company came in especially to see him and was very supportive.

He reported that throughout the first week he was generally withdrawn and was unable to concentrate on anything. In his usual routine he would have read and watched television but he found these activities particularly difficult. He was restless and made excuses to go for short walks, especially at times when he was unlikely to meet people he knew. He had become very distressed when a friend asked him about the accident and was anxious to avoid repeating this experience. His wife encouraged him to start driving again as soon as possible. Initially he resisted but on the Monday he drove three miles to his GP and back, accompanied by his wife. He was very vigilant and drove with great caution.

He reported that he had four consultations with the counsellor at his GP's surgery over the first month and found these helpful. He reported that she encouraged him to continue driving and helped him to re-evaluate his sense of being responsible for the accident. He said that during the second week he felt more relaxed after his first consultation and was endeavouring at that stage to believe and accept that the accident and the deaths of the victims had not been his fault. He said that during the second week he, nevertheless, felt generally on edge and that although there was some improvement he 'still became distressed and tearful'. He reported that at that stage he was still withdrawn, did not wish to answer the telephone, could not make decisions, felt a general loss of confidence and did not wish to have any responsibilities.

He said that during the second week he became increasingly short tempered and that he became snappy with his wife and children and intolerant towards other road users. He reported that intrusive thoughts and flashbacks of the accident still occurred several times a day but that as the second week progressed his ability to concentrate improved. He had begun driving again during the first week and then continued to drive daily. Initially it needed his wife's encouragement to do this but by the end of the first week, he was taking the decision to drive and driving his car alone. He was initially very cautious and vigilant but as time passed he said that he became less cautious at the wheel though more angry and less tolerant of other drivers than prior to the accident.

He returned to work four weeks after the accident after arranging to have a preliminary drive of a heavy goods vehicle (HGV) just before returning to work. He wanted to see how he would cope with driving a HGV again. He said that when he first drove a HGV that he felt very apprehensive, drove slowly and cautiously, was very aware of all the traffic around him and checked the mirrors 'much more than usual'.

At the time he returned to work he reported that he had made further improvement and had stopped his sessions with the counsellor. He reported that he had made substantial gains over the month. He said that by this stage he was usually sleeping on average 6 hours a night but that his sleep was broken by bad dreams of the accident about three times a week after which it would take him an hour to settle and return to sleep. He noted that he still became tearful about twice a week, usually in response to people enquiring about the accident. He reported that he could feel that his confidence had improved by the end of the month but was not yet back to normal. He no longer wanted to avoid the company of people other than his close family and had started to meet up with friends to play darts or dominos and 'have a pint'. His friends attempted to protect him from being questioned about the accident as far as possible. By the end of the month he noticed that he was less distressed if someone mentioned the accident and that it had become easier to talk about it.

A month after the accident intrusive thoughts occurred once or twice a day and he said that after these he 'felt sad' for about 30 minutes. Flashbacks occurred two or three times a week although these were not as previously. It would still take him about 15 to 30 minutes to settle and regain his composure after these occurred. His concentration remained variable and, he reported, he became aware of being absent-minded and forgetful, especially over appointments or arrangements to meet someone. The medical notes mention one missed counselling appointment when he arrived at the correct time but one day late. In public places, he often felt that everyone knew that he was the person who had been involved in 'the accident'. He also knew that this was ridiculous and with gradually increasing success could talk himself out of this sense of being watched. He noted that he continued to be irritable at home and on the roads and to be cautious and vigilant when driving.

He said that his general sense of anxiety increased before he returned to work. The atmosphere at work is friendly and there is a lot of good-natured teasing. He did not feel ready to cope with this especially in relation to the accident. In the event he found that his colleagues were sensitive and supportive. Someone he had not known very well previously talked about his experience of a fatal accident some years earlier. He no longer felt as alone with the experience and realised that his colleagues wanted him back. For the first week he avoided driving the vehicle that had been involved in the accident but this meant driving unfamiliar routes and on the second week back he resumed driving the same vehicle he had driven prior to the accident and on the same route. This meant passing the accident site several times a day. He had managed to avoid it in the car but there were no suitable alternative routes for a large vehicle. He found this difficult when he approached the site for the first time and saw the remains of flowers and wreaths on the verge. He pulled over into a lay-by to cry. After that the worst was over. Every time he passed the site in the first week he felt sad for the lost lives of the young people and their grieving relatives. He was relieved when the grass was cut and the flowers removed over the next weekend. He noticed that by the third week he was sometimes driving past the site without noticing and was relieved that his mind was now wholly on driving that stretch of road. The sense of anxious over-awareness when he drives that stretch of road has persisted to the time of the interview.

Presentation at the time of interview

At the time of interview he reported that he was physically well.

He said that he had spells of being low in spirits for a few hours and that these occurred once a fortnight. He considered that these might be brought on by reminders of the accident and might, at least in part, be his feelings of sadness at the loss of life in the accident of people only a little older than his children. He was able to report that his sleep was normal and that bad dreams no longer occurred, having stopped within two months of the accident. He said that he was able to relax and was not generally tense or anxious and said that though he continued to be more irritable than he had been in the past that his irritability had improved over the months since the accident.

He indicated that he still found it difficult to concentrate for any length of time and still suffered with absent-mindedness. He said that previously he had been good at recalling and passing on messages but that now he had to write them down and even then could forget to pass them on. He was getting better at keeping appointments but he was aware of finding it more of an effort than before the accident to keep appointments and he continued to miss some occasionally. He reported that he was socialising regularly and was back to enjoying the company of his 'mates' but was less outgoing with people he did not know than previously. He had lost confidence and relied more on his wife to make important decisions about his family and work life. He seldom thought of the accident spontaneously unless something reminded him of it. When this occurred, usually about twice a week, his feelings and thoughts were no longer as intense and lasted for a shorter period of time, typically 10–15 minutes.

He reported that he drove a car most days and said that he was able to drive any distance and on any road. He admitted to being bad tempered with other road users and intolerant of bad driving but considered that he was less angry on the roads than he had been in the early months after the accident. He reported that at the wheel of his car he felt relaxed and confident and was able to enjoy driving again much of the time. It was no longer an ordeal although he remains more vigilant and has a heightened awareness of junctions joining dual carriageways from the right.

He considered that he was more vigilant when driving a HGV than a car. He was aware of using his mirrors and watching junctions more than was strictly required to drive safely. He was able to drive past the scene of the accident without significant difficulty. Any negative feelings were more likely to occur when the roads were quiet. He had become able to divide his attention between the road and the radio in his cab which had not been possible when he first returned to work.

He reported that he travelled as a passenger about once a week and had no difficulty in being a passenger. He also indicated that he had no problems when he was a pedestrian.

Psychological Measures

The Beck Depression Scale Second Edition (BDI-II)[1] and the Impact of Event Scale (IES)[2] were administered. The BDI is a self-report instrument for measuring the severity of depression and the IES is a self-report measure of specific responses to trauma. On the BDI-II he scored 13 and on the IES he scored 6 for Intrusion and 6 for Avoidance. These scores indicate a mild but not clinically significant degree of depressed mood and both relatively low levels of intrusive thoughts and relatively mild degrees of suppression of trauma-related phenomena.

History and circumstances

He said that he had only been involved in one previous road traffic accident which had been a minor accident, when he was aged 26, in which he had suffered no physical injuries or psychological sequelae. He did note that he had suffered a knee injury in 1999 after falling off a trailer tailgate in the course of his work. He had keyhole surgery to repair a cartilage. He reported that he made a very good recovery after this operation.

He acknowledged that he had suffered from an episode of depression in 1994 following family difficulties concerning his 16-year-old daughter. He changed his work pattern to be more available at home but missed his usual colleagues. The depression eased over a few months and cleared when he resumed his usual routine. He could not recall any other depressive episodes.

He has been married for 26 years and has two adult children aged 21 and 23. After six years in the army, he has worked as a HGV driver for 17 years, and has been with his current employer for nine years.

Medical Record

His medical record refers to him having been depressed in 1994 'due to family difficulties'. A course of mild anti-depressants were prescribed for three months. On 12 June 1996 it is noted that he was 'getting depressed again over last 1/12'. On 23 July 1996 it is noted: 'feeling a little better in himself – sleeping and eating returning to normal' and on 11 November 1996: 'returned to usual work – greatly improved mood. Family difficulties more settled'.

Opinion

The accident in question was a severe accident which resulted in the deaths of two young people slightly older than his children. It is evident that this was an extremely distressing experience for Mr Rydal. He required the help of a nurse in the A&E Department immediately after the accident, and some sessions from a counsellor in the first month, in order to start to come to terms with the trauma.

Immediately after the impact he showed signs of being dissociated and subsequently suffered from a range of symptoms of post-traumatic stress including re-experiencing phenomena in the form of intrusive thoughts, flashbacks and disturbing dreams of the accident; numbing/avoidance phenomena in the form of social withdrawal, diminished interest in activities and a constricted range of emotions; and hyper-arousal phenomena in the form of anxiety, irritability, sleep disturbance, hyper-vigilance and concentration difficulties. In addition he became cautious and vigilant when driving and intolerant of inconsiderate drivers on the roads.

He was acutely disturbed over the first few weeks and required a month off work. There was a trend of improvement within a few days of the accident and he benefited from his sessions with a counsellor. By the end of the first month, he had significantly improved and took the step of returning to work and one week after his return was driving the same vehicle which he had been driving at the time of the accident.

At the time of assessment, eight months after the accident, he had made further gains and there was a continuing trend of improvement. He was able to relax and to sleep normally. Though he was still vigilant driving a car, and cautious when driving a Heavy Goods Vehicle, he was able to drive without significant difficulty. He had some persisting irritability and occasional low moods, suffered with absent-mindedness and occasional intrusive thoughts and complained that his concentration was not as good as it had been prior to the accident.

It would be appropriate to conclude that he suffered with an Acute Stress Disorder, according to the diagnostic criteria of the *Diagnostic and Statistical Manual of Mental Disorders* 4th Edition (DSM-IV),[3] as a consequence of the accident in question. The constellation of symptoms was not of duration to fulfil the full criteria for a diagnosis of Post-Traumatic Stress Disorder.

He has made good progress considering the nature of the trauma and it is to his credit that he sought immediate help for his emotional difficulties. It is still only eight months since the accident and it would be expected that he will continue to improve and largely overcome his residual difficulties over the next 12 months.

He was advised to have further sessions with the counsellor he saw previously or a Clinical Psychologist, should his residual difficulties become troublesome or the continuing trend of improvement cease prior to full recovery.

I understand that in preparing this report that my duty is to the court and I consider that I have complied with that duty. I believe that the facts that I have stated are true and that the opinions I have expressed are correct.

Yours faithfully

C. S. Rydal B.A., D.Clin. Psych., C.Psychol., A.F.B.Ps.S.D.
Consultant Clinical Psychologist

1 Beck Depression Inventory Second Edition (1996) *The Psychological Corporation*. San Antonio: Harcourt Brace & Co.
2 Horowitz, M. I., Wilner, N. and Alvarez, M. A. (1979) Impact of Event Scale: A measure of subjective stress. *Psychosomatic Medicine*. Vol. 41, No. 3.
3 American Psychiatric Association (1994) *Diagnostic and Statistical Manual of Mental Disorders*. Fourth Edition. Washington, DC: American Psychiatric Association.

Criminal injury compensation claim reports

Compensation is available to individuals or groups of people who suffer a personal injury arising out of a crime or act of negligence committed by another person. The events resulting in a claim to the Criminal Injury Compensation Authority (CICA) may have caused the victim to suffer from a number of conditions, including psychological damage, post-traumatic stress disorder, depression and trauma. As a result, some victims may have sought therapy for such problems and may want their therapist to write a report for them in support of a compensation claim.

The request for a report can come from different sources:

- From the client.
- From the client's solicitor.
- From the Criminal Injury Compensation Authority (CICA), who would make contact with the therapist directly.
- From a private solicitor (acting on behalf of either the claimant or defendant) who refers the individual to the independent therapist for the sole purpose of obtaining an assessment in support of or against a claim.

The initial report is usually by way of completing a questionnaire. If CICA want more information or something clarified they will usually contact the practitioner with further questions. See Chapter 8 for more information relating to this.

Pre-sentence reports

Pre-sentence reports are ordered by the court and generally made by a probation officer or social worker. The purpose of the report is to assist the court in deciding the most suitable method of dealing with the offender. These reports will be ordered before:

- Imposing any custodial sentence.
- Making a community punishment order and rehabilitation order.
- Making a drug treatment and testing order.

Requests for these types of reports are more likely to arise in settings where therapists are working with offenders and are likely to come from the client's probation officer. There are increasing numbers of requests made directly by lawyers representing the client for use in mitigation to argue for lowest possible sentence. The client may have also suggested that their therapist would be the ideal person to provide insight into the client's personal issues and present any contributing factors that have led them to commit a crime. The following is an example of such a report:

Therapeutic evidence in the case of A. N. Offer

From: G. Edwards

Wessex Hospital
Avon Road
Seven City

1 February 2005

A. N. Offer DOB 15.07.1965

I have been asked to provide relevant information regarding the above-named client. I understand that this information will be referred to in relation to criminal proceedings against the client and is provided at the client's own request to assist the court.

I confirm that I have been counselling this client for anxiety for the past two years. I have seen this client for three series of six sessions. The last session completed six weeks ago. The client can be described as suffering from severe mood swings, from feelings of euphoria to feelings of deep anxiety and dread. The work with the client has involved an exploration of why these feelings have come to exist and how they can be overcome.

Present Condition

The client reported being repeatedly upset by contact with her former partner which frequently triggers feelings of overwhelming anxiety. At the time of the offence, she was going through a particularly difficult time as she informed me that her partner had threatened to take custody of her son. As a result she was under a great deal of pressure and it is likely that this was a contributing factor to her commiting the offence.

[Signed by therapist]

Coroners' reports

Coroners or, in Scotland, the Procurator Fiscal in charge of a Fatal Accident Inquiry may request a report from a therapist where the deceased had been receiving counselling. Requests for such reports will usually come via a formal letter or a telephone call from the coroner's/fiscal office (Dorries, 1999: 128). Although therapists are under no obligation to prepare a statement or report, the coroner/fiscal may suggest it as a preferable alternative to appearing as a witness, or as a way of helping to identify permissible questions from interested parties. Therapists are like any other witnesses in this respect. Refusal is not open to any direct sanction, nor is such refusal a common law obstruction of the coroner. However, if a therapist does refuse to provide the report and the coroner/fiscal believes it necessary for the inquest, the coroner/fiscal can require that the therapist attends court to give oral evidence, which they must do when directed to do so. Attendance can be compelled through a witness summons and, if you fail to attend in response to a witness summons, you can be arrested and brought before the coroner/fiscal in custody for a penalty to be imposed.

There are some basic guidelines for writing a report for the coroner's court/fatal accident inquiry:

- It is essential to have contemporaneous notes available for reference, when writing the report.
- It should deal with matters relevant to the inquest in chronological order.
- It must be factual, written with care and free of ambiguous language.
- It should include a summary, conclusion and an element of opinion (Dorries, 1999: 130). However, there are no strict rules to follow when writing this type of report. It can include fact and/or opinion and may include history of the work with the client.

Like with any report, the author has a duty not to mislead the coroner's court/fatal accident inquiry. A criminal case in 1994 established that deliberately misleading an inquest could amount to 'perverting the course of justice' (*R v. Sinha*, 1994). Here a doctor was said to have falsified records to make it appear that he was not at fault for a death.

Chapter summary

- In following the general principles that apply to preparing reports, therapists will achieve a report that is clear, objective and adequately conveys what they intend it to.
- You need to know the different formalities with regard to the differing reports and statements:

  - A witness statement, most commonly taken down by the police, generally contains factual information.
  - Expert reports are prepared by individuals who are at the top end of their profession and writers need to ensure the utmost impartiality so that their overriding duty is to the court. Ensure you have received a full and comprehensive list of instructions from the solicitor; for example on what areas to report on and for which type of court proceedings the report is for. Care should be taken so that the report is written by taking into account the requirements of civil, criminal and family proceedings.

- When considering whether or not to write criminal injury compensation reports, therapists need to consider things like who the request is coming from and carry out an assessment of the various factors that might interfere with the therapeutic relationship as a result of writing the report.
- Requests for pre-sentence reports are more likely to occur in settings where therapists are working with offenders and will normally come from the client's probation officer. The example presented earlier is a realistic indication of the kind of thing courts will require.
- Writing a report for the coroner's court/fatal accident inquiry may be a preferable alternative to attending court to give oral evidence. When writing the report, ensure you use contemporaneous notes to inform the writing and that you do not mislead the court in any way.

The example of a psychological report provided as an expert witness report written by a psychologist follows the conventions of writing this type of report but the content is fictional and does not represent the actual experience of any particular organisation or individual.

Appearing as a Witness

Being asked to give evidence can be a daunting prospect for therapists, especially as the law frequently requires that any fact, which needs to be proved, is to be established by giving oral evidence in public, particularly in criminal cases. The transparency of this style stands in direct opposition to the way in which therapists approach their work. Therapy is more about taking time to talk and working through issues, generally over a long period of time. Trials on the other hand involve presenting succinct verbal arguments in open court. For example, they are rarely objective inquiries into past events, but adversarial contests in which parties, who have a vested interest in the outcome, not only decide what evidence they wish to present or prevent from being presented, but also present it in as persuasive a manner as possible.

A situation may therefore occur which could require your counselling notes and content of sessions to be examined by a court at some time in the future; in such cases you can be compelled to attend as a witness. One of the purposes of a judicial trial is to establish a true version of events and the court can compel your attendance if it feels that without your evidence a fair trial would not be possible.

The aim of this chapter is to enable therapists to understand their role in relation to the courts and appearing as a witness. Requests to appear as a witness can be for the mainstream court system or for the coroner's court. There are some clear distinctions between the two court systems and the way in which oral evidence is to be given; this chapter provides guidance on giving evidence in both settings. A distinction is also made between appearance in court as a lay witness of fact and an expert witness.

The Mainstream Court System

This section concerns appearing as a witness in criminal and civil courts, not coroners court.

Witness of fact

Initially it is important to distinguish between being a witness of fact and an expert witness. A witness of fact is someone who is called to give evidence about what happened in a case. They are asked to recall what they saw or heard during an incident but not to give opinions. There is a requirement to discuss the facts they remember or have recorded in notes. An obvious example is a doctor who may record details of a patient's injuries. In the context of counselling a therapist may say that a client was present at a specified time and date for the purpose of counselling. Evidence of facts also include those which therapists have observed, for example, handwriting, a broken leg, skid marks on a road and those things that have been told, for instance, the level of pain, mental injury caused or facts observed from documents.

If you refuse to act as a witness of fact, you can be compelled to do so. A party, or their lawyer, who is relying on you to attend court can ask the court to issue a Form N20 (witness summons). The following is an example of the witness summons that can be served to enforce your attendence in court in England.

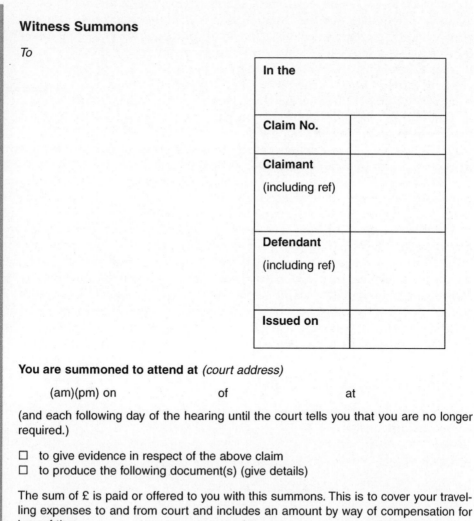

Witness Summons

To

In the	
Claim No.	
Claimant (including ref)	
Defendant (including ref)	
Issued on	

You are summoned to attend at *(court address)*

(am)(pm) on   of   at

(and each following day of the hearing until the court tells you that you are no longer required.)

☐   to give evidence in respect of the above claim
☐   to produce the following document(s) (give details)

The sum of £ is paid or offered to you with this summons. This is to cover your travelling expenses to and from court and includes an amount by way of compensation for loss of time.

This summons was issued on the application of the claimant (defendant) or the claimant's (defendant's) solicitor whose name, address and reference number is:

Do not ignore this summons

If you were offered money for travel expenses and compensation for loss of time, at that time it was served on you, and you

- Fail to attend or produce documents as required by the summons; or
- Refuse to take an oath or affirm for the purpose of answering questions about your evidence or the documents you have been asked to produce

You may be liable to a fine or imprisonment and may in addition be ordered to pay any costs resulting from your failure to attend or refusal to take an oath or affirm.

Certificate of service

Claim No.	

I certify that the summons of which this is a true copy, was served by posting to _____ (the witness) on _____ at the address stated on the summons in accordance with the request of the applicant or his solicitor.

I enclosed a P.O. for £ for the witness's expenses and compensation for loss of time.

Signed _____
Officer of the Court

In Scotland you will receive a witness citation. This form/citation informs you that you must comply and act as a witness. The summons will include details of when and where to attend. If you still refuse to attend, you will be in 'contempt of court' and can be fined up to £1,000. If a witness summons is received but you are unable to attend the hearing, you can apply to have the summons withdrawn. Before doing this, contact the relevant party or their solicitor. They may be able to help with any difficulty you have in attending.

If they cannot assist, the therapist should go to the court where the summons was issued as soon as possible and ask to have their arguments for refusal to attend to be put to the judge. A fee may be required for this. An appointment is then given to see a judge, who listens to your reasons and any objections, and decides if you should be excused from acting as a witness. The person who issued the summons can attend and present counter arguments. Therapists would be advised to consider carefully before making this application, as if it is unsuccessful, they may have to pay the costs of the party who issued the witness summons. It is always useful to know that if a party is aware of your reluctance to attend court and give evidence, it may be risky for them to compel you to do so, as they will be unsure about what you will say. In such circumstances they can apply to the court without notice for an order to serve a 'witness summary'. This would require you to provide a witness summary of your evidence as a written record. Further guidance will usually be provided at the time.

In Scotland, if you are a witness of fact and have a good reason for not being able to attend on the date given in your citation, you can request to be allowed to give your evidence at a different time, either before the court proceedings take place, or during them. The party seeking to call you as a witness and who wants to rely upon your evidence will usually try and arrange for this to be done.

In circumstances where you are employed full time and you are willing to attend but your employer refuses to give you time off work, you can request a witness summon or a citation to be sent to you, which can be shown to your employers when considering your request for time off.

Expert witness

Expert opinion is allowed on matters not within the common knowledge of the court. Professionals, particularly individuals from the medical profession, are regularly consulted by solicitors for their expert opinions about matters relevant to anticipated litigation. This is because the court needs help in knowing or under-standing matters within certain fields of expertise. For example, where a referral of a victim has been made to an independent therapist, he or she may comment that the client was demonstrating certain behaviour during the counselling session, about which the therapist can provide an opinion.

Expert witnesses should be individuals with qualifications and experience which equip them to give opinions on the facts of the case. A therapist who is called to give evidence in an expert capacity needs to ensure their independence from the case, despite being paid by one of the parties to give evidence. If the expert witness is also the treating therapist, which may occur in proceedings relating to children but is less likely in other types of case, the therapist needs to adopt an impartial and objective perspective. The role of the expert is that of an independent educator, helping the court to reach a fair decision. Evidence from expert witnesses will normally be required in two forms; a written report and oral evidence given in the witness box.

You can refuse to act as an expert witness. You need to decide whether you can spare time from your work to prepare a report and/or attend a hearing. Aim to tell the party or their acting solicitor as soon as possible if you have something arranged, for example a holiday or hospital appointment, which may affect the dates you can attend court.

Competence and independence

There is no fixed test to qualify as an expert witness and anyone who has special expertise in an area can be considered as an expert. Therapists, therefore, need to reflect on whether they feel they have the relevant qualifications and practical experience in the field in question. The law also makes it very clear that the duty of an expert is to help the court on matters within their expertise and this duty overrides any obligation to the person from whom they have received instructions or by whom they have been paid. Consider the following scenario in relation to this:

> Tim has been referred to Ann for assessment of post-traumatic stress disorder as a result of injuries sustained at work. She has been asked to appear as an independent expert witness by his insurance company. The instructing solicitor has requested that the assessment should concentrate specifically on the post-traumatic stress disorder. However, Ann believes that Tim is also in a lot of physical pain as a result of his injuries and would like to express this in her evidence to the court.

Ann is insufficiently independent to take on the role of expert witness in this situation for this type of case. A truly independent report involving an assessment of the person concerned will be viewed much more favourably by the court. Ann's contribution to the case is more likely to be as witness of fact. The independent expert may also request to see Ann's case records or request a brief report of the work undertaken with her client which will be referred to as one of the sources of evidence from which the facts are constructed. For an example of this see the psychologist's report in Chapter 3.

What am I required to do when approached by a solicitor to be an expert witness?

In the initial contact, whether by telephone or a meeting, therapists will be asked probing questions about qualifications and previous court experience. Lack of court experience does not necessarily mean that you are not a suitable candidate, as expertise in the field is more important.

As an expert witness, the therapist has a working contract with the solicitor and not the client. Communications between the expert and solicitor are protected by privilege from being seen by anyone but the instructing solicitor and the client. Once the decision has been reached to use the evidence in court, the solicitor will reveal the contents of the report to the other side.

You need to be proactive in getting all the necessary information and instructions from the solicitor and establish what area of practice they require your expertise in. The following would need to be discussed with the solicitor:

- Whether the solicitor needs a preliminary report, a final report or both.
- Knowing what stage the case is at and information on the main issues in the case.

- Establishing the deadlines for writing a report and the fee.
- Viewing court documents, photographs, diagrams and witness statements.
- Clarifying and explaining complex technical areas to the solicitor.

Detailed investigation and research into the facts of the case is important. Therefore, gather all the facts and build a foundation upon which to base an opinion. Paying close attention to the following will enable you to be fully prepared in giving expert evidence:

- Ensuring all the available information has been obtained from the solicitors. You should be proactive in obtaining documents.
- Creating a working relationship with solicitors, to assist in understanding what is required from him or her. A meeting with the barrister or in Scotland an advocate may be required if the case is particularly complex; sometimes known as a 'conference with counsel'. This may be important in order to discuss the relationship between the expert evidence and the legal issues being raised in the case.
- Ensuring the expert report is independent and objective.
- Identifying the strengths and weaknesses of the case, considering all the possible arguments, for instance the likely questions that will be put in cross-examination (see p. 67).
- Ensuring notes and files are in good order and correctly paginated. This will help you to remain in control of the evidence.
- Familiarising yourself with the documents, by re-reading notes and the report. It is important to be able to find your way around the report quickly and accurately. A chronology will assist with this.

What are expert witness meetings and when would it be appropriate to hold one?

It may be appropriate to hold a 'without prejudice' meeting between experts for the purpose of discussing complex issues and theories relating to the issues in the case. It would involve the therapists pooling information and thoughts together, and identifying areas where further investigation is required. A greater level of understanding of the issues and experts' reasoning can be acquired through this process.

There are two types of meetings:

1 The **first is that ordered by the court** in civil proceedings, which means that what is said or agreed between experts cannot be used in evidence at the subsequent trial. The parties involved or their respective solicitors may not be present during such meetings.
2 The **second is agreed between the parties** and is a meeting of experts, together with the parties involved and their solicitors, at any time before or during the trial. The parties themselves define the object of the meeting.

   It is more appropriate for this type of meeting to take place in private without involvement of solicitors. Where solicitors are in attendance it is only in the capacity of an observer and not one of participation in the discussions.

   The meeting will involve the following:

- Preparation of a chronological statement of facts with a summary of important or disputed points.
- An agreed agenda, listing the areas of dispute.
- A report detailing the agreed matters of professional opinion plus issues that are still in dispute to be submitted at the end of the meeting. Both agreed and disagreed matters should be noted.

What are the common pitfalls to avoid when acting as an expert witness?

Therapists are responsible for their own evidence and research carried out into the facts. If your opinion is considered to be biased by the party instructing you, or in some other way of little value, another therapist may be instructed to give evidence in your place. If that does not happen and you proceed to give evidence that is impaired by poor preparation or bias, you risk prejudicing the case of the party by whom you have been instructed and paid. If insufficient investigations have been carried out or bias is reflected in their opinion, there is also the risk that you are found to be in breach of contract or to have acted negligently. Some clients are also using professional conduct procedures to complain about incompetently produced expert witness reports.

The common problems and pitfalls in relation to expert witnesses can be divided into the general and the specific:

General

- Inadequate instructions from a solicitor.
- Failure to deliver independent or impartial advice. Ensure it is the therapist's opinion and not the solicitor's or that of anyone else.
- Failure or lack of communication between the solicitor and the expert.
- Failure to have a written contract which agrees what service the therapist is providing for the instructing solicitors.
- Breaching confidentiality and defamation of an individual in the report.
- Technical errors.
- Failing to acknowledge other possibilities.

Specific

- If therapists find themselves involved in preparing a joint statement, they need to ensure that their views are properly and clearly stated and not lost in the body of the report (*Youssef* v. *Jordan*, 2003). The judgment is reinforced by the Civil Procedure Rules 1998 which state that in the event of a joint expert witness report being prepared, and following a discussion between experts, they must prepare a statement for the court showing the following:

  - Those issues on which they agree, and
  - those issues on which they disagree and a summary of their reasons for disagreeing (Civil Procedure Rules, 1998 Part 35.12).

- In *Wardlaw* v. *Farrar* (2003) an expert relied on a section of the *Oxford Textbook of Medicine*. In addition to not being copied to the other expert, an incomplete extract from the textbook was copied and presented at trial. Insufficient instructions relating to the exchange of list of articles and books were also given by the court. The judge held that directions should routinely be given in relation to exchange of literature. It is advisable to keep lists of relevant documentation and ask your instructing solicitor if he or she will be forwarding them to the other party's solicitor.
- In *Devoran Joinery Co. Ltd* v. *Perkins* (2003) the claimant's expert was criticised for admitting a mistake under cross-examination. The judge commented that he should clearly have corrected his report before that point in time, indeed before he went into the witness box. If you change your view after producing a report, this should be communicated to all the parties without delay and, when appropriate, to the court. Changing your opinion late in the day is permissible but you should correct your witness statement as soon as possible, not leaving it until you are being cross-examined, otherwise it will be perceived to be less than credible. In Scotland, witness statements are not prepared, but you should advise the solicitor instructing you if you change your opinion from that which is set out in your report.
- Any document referred to in a witness statement or expert evidence must be disclosed. See *Lucas* v. *Barking, Havering and Redbridge Hospitals NHS Trust*, 2003, where an expert was supplied with specific documents to be used as basis for advice, the other party to the case can require these documents to be disclosed. The objective of this is to ensure that evidence is accurate and complete.
- The defendants in *Beck* v. *Ministry of Defence* (2003) lost confidence in the expert and applied for permission to appoint a new expert. It was held that the original report should be disclosed, as this would discourage 'expert shopping' and it would ensure that the claimant did not think that the real reason why defendants wanted a new expert was because the first report had been favourable to the claimant. In Scotland, if a party chooses to instruct a new expert, then on the whole they are entitled to do so and there would be no requirement to disclose the existing report.

To avoid the pitfalls discussed above and claims of professional negligence and breach of contract of services, you should seek to:

- Demonstrate that reasonable care and skill is exercised in the course of being an expert. Keeping comprehensive notes of what occurred and what was said will help you to achieve this.
- Keep yourself updated through training, research and supervision. A commitment to good practice requires therapists to keep up to date with the latest knowledge. Regularly monitoring and reviewing one's work is essential not only for the purposes of ensuring expert evidence is of a high quality, but also for maintaining good practice.
- Be clear in the advice that is provided and ensure that solicitors are kept informed.
- Keep all notes relating to the case for at least six years. Breach of contract cases can be brought for up to six years after the breach is discovered, and negligence cases can be brought up to three years from the date it was realised that the negligent act occurred.

How to prepare for court?

Therapists may be apprehensive about appearing in court, either as a witness of fact or an expert witness. However, with careful preparation and by following some simple guidelines, the process can become less daunting. As with many challenges, it is the preparation which is all important. Therapists who are attending as expert witnesses are likely to have attended court beforehand. If this is not the case, the information outlined in this chapter provides a basic introduction to giving evidence as an expert witness. If therapists are planning to undertake expert witness work on a regular basis, then they would benefit from attending a training course specifically for this, which may be beneficial in understanding the practical aspects of performing this role.

If you are attending court for the very first time, it may be helpful to visit and become familiar with the surroundings. Every court has a Customer Service Officer who will be pleased, when requested to do so, to send out a leaflet indicating the location of the court and describing its facilities. It is important to be clear about the time, date and place of the hearing. By contacting the Customer Service Officer of the court concerned, arrangements can also be made to go inside the courtroom and even into the witness box where evidence will be given. In England arrangements can also be made via the court witness programme to sit in on a court hearing so that a sense of the layout and procedure can be ascertained. In Scotland, the majority of court proceedings are open to the public, so it should be possible to sit in during a case in order to familiarise yourself with the process. Initial information about being a witness in the English courts can be obtained from the Court Service website. In Scotland, information can be found on the Scottish courts' website at www.scotcourts.gov.uk.

You may also enquire from the courts or the solicitors how long the trial or hearing is scheduled to last and the length of time for which you will be expected to give evidence. Ensure your diary has been cleared, and any counselling sessions have been re-scheduled and clients have been made aware of the extent of your unavailability. A suitable form of dress should be worn, for example smart, subdued, professional clothes – dark suits, plain shirts and blouses are advisable. It is important to feel comfortable and professional and not look out of place in a courtroom.

Before attending court ensure you have read through all the original notes, statement and/or report (as well as any relevant reports lodged by the other party to the court case) to refresh your memory of all the issues. All the papers relating to the case will need to be on hand and they should all be in the right order so that they can be referred to quickly and easily.

The order of proceedings at the court hearing or trial

You should seek to arrive at court early and meet the solicitors, and find out where the waiting room and any other refreshment facilities are located. Examine the list of cases in the waiting area. The list will say whether the case will be heard in public or in private. It should also include the name of the judge and whether he or she is a High Court, Circuit or District Judge. In Scotland, the type of judge hearing the case will depend upon whether the case is being heard in the Sheriff Court, the High Court or the Court of Session. Before going into court, you will be asked to inform the court usher of the holy book on which you wish to swear the oath. It is possible to choose affirmation, which is a promise to tell the truth without any reference to religious belief.

Expert witnesses are allowed to sit in court and observe, while witnesses of facts have to wait outside the courtroom. In Scotland, however, a party seeking to have their expert sit in court and listen to evidence will have to ask the permission of the court. Check with the solicitor as to whom you may or may not talk to. If it is necessary to leave the waiting area for any reason, you should inform the usher immediately.

In court the judge is seated on a raised platform behind a bench. In criminal trials in the Crown Court, or the Sheriff Court or High Court in Scotland, there is a jury as well as a judge, sitting in a separate area. In the Magistrates Court there are three lay magistrates (non-legal professionals). Tribunals consist of three people, usually including one who is legally qualified. The clerks and officials sit directly in front of the judge or magistrates, with the witness box at the side of the room and usually raised. The solicitors and barristers/advocates are situated behind tables facing the bench, with the expert witnesses seated behind the barristers/advocates.

Before witnesses are called, the legal representatives make an opening speech explaining their version of the events. The claimant's representative presents his or her case and the claimant's witnesses are called to the witness box and each is questioned by their legal representative and cross-examined by the defence. The defence then presents its case, calling its witnesses for examination and cross-examination (see p. 67).

The court usher calls out the witness's name when it is time for them to give evidence. The witness is shown to the witness box and asked to swear (take an oath) or affirm to tell the truth. The oath is a promise on the Bible, or other holy book, to tell the truth, while an affirmation is solemn promise to tell the truth. Both carry equal weight. If the hearing is in the judge's chambers, there is no witness box and the witnesses normally sit around a large table together with others involved in the case.

The legal representatives then summarise the evidence that is presented in a closing speech. The judge or magistrates then gives the decision. In a criminal trial, the judge will give a summation of evidence and the jury retires to consider its verdict. When the verdict is returned, the judge will either pass sentence or release, or defer sentence until pre-sentence reports are produced.

How to give evidence on the witness stand

Witnesses of fact cannot take notes into the witness box, although they may be asked to look at their statement; whereas expert witnesses are allowed to look at their reports. However, permission to refer to notes is requested by the solicitor or barrister/advocate and granted by the judge. Notes or documents for use in a trial are contained in the court bundle and, as mentioned earlier, court officers call witnesses into court when they are needed. When answering questions, the witness should turn towards the judge and then give their answer. This will help you to focus more clearly and prevent you from being tempted to get into a conversation with the legal representative asking you questions.

Examination-in-chief

This is the process whereby a witness is questioned by the legal representative who has called them as a witness. The examination need not be confined to the witness statement or expert report and may relate to any matters relevant to the issue, which appear to be within the competence and knowledge of the witness. The process will begin with the therapist giving their name and professional address.

Expert witnesses will also be asked to give their qualifications, experience and area of expertise. In criminal cases, witnesses may be asked many questions in order to bring out the evidence in the report. Whereas in civil cases, the judge may have already read the report and will merely want confirmation that it is accurate and up-to-date.

Cross-examination

This is where the opposition's legal representation will question the witness. The purpose of a cross-examination is partly to elicit facts that may be of value to the opposing party's case, and partly to challenge the witness's evidence and standing. Barristers/advocates may appear to attack the witness personally, to discredit them and to destroy or reduce their credibility. This is known as 'impeachment', and is perfectly permissible. It is not advisable to get into an argument with the barrister/advocate, or react angrily or defensively. Try to remain helpful, restrained, down to earth, but certain of the case as you wish to present it. However, therapists should note that an attack on the credibility of their evidence is highly unlikely in proceedings involving children in the Family Division of the court. Judges, in such cases, need all the available information relating to the case in order to make a decision which is in the best interests of the child. As a result, witnesses in the Family Court are treated with respect and courtesy.

Re-examination

This does not always take place in a hearing but is an option for the legal representative if they wish to have something clarified or to remind the court of the significance of the evidence that has been given.

The witness is informed that he or she can leave the witness box.

What does the judge expect from therapists in their capacity as an expert witness?

The judge approaches the evidence of an expert witness by examining the reasons given for his or her opinions and the extent to which they are supported by the evidence. The legal representative of each party will then want to ask questions. In responding, therapists need to speak clearly, directing their answers to the judge or magistrates and not to the person who is asking the questions. Answers should be given clearly and not too quickly as the judge and others are taking notes of the evidence. The speed and presentation of evidence in general is vital. Keeping sentences short, simple and logical, as well as avoiding technical language, helps the evidence to be delivered in a professional manner. The judge or magistrates will note the following with regard to expert evidence:

- The precision and accuracy of thought as demonstrated by the answers.
- The response to searching and informed cross-examination.
- The extent to which a witness faces up to and accepts the logic of a proposition put in cross-examination or is prepared to defend valid opinions or concede points that are seen to be incorrect.

The judiciary want to ensure that the correct decision is reached and, as a result, they need to be able to trust an expert witness in helping them to come to the right decision. Therefore, therapists should ensure that their evidence is impartial and honest, and conveyed in their capacity as an independent professional.

Modes of address in different courts

When entering the unfamiliar environment of the court system, therapists would be well equipped to have an awareness of the different modes of addressing a judge or magistrate in each of the different courts. If appearing as witness, your answers will need to be directed at whoever is sitting on the case. Therefore, in complying with the legal etiquette of the courtroom, the individual sitting on a case will need to be addressed in the appropriate manner. The following chart illustrates which judge will be presiding on a case in the relevant court and how they should be addressed throughout the legal proceedings.

The Coroner's Court

There is difficulty in providing guidance relating to the coroner's court, as there is variation in both practice and procedure from court to court. This is as a result of the traditional independence of coroners and the permitted variations in the ways in which they exercise their powers. The purpose of this section is to assist and guide therapists who come into contact with the coroner's court and become involved in the investigation of the death of their client.

It has become common practice for therapists to be called to give evidence in the coroner's court, especially where there is the possibility that the client has committed suicide. This is a particularly challenging situation. Quite apart from any feelings the therapist may have about the death of their client, they will be faced with decisions relating as to what to disclose about their client's intentions. These disclosures may need to be made in the unfamiliar environment of the court room,

England and Wales

Court	Who sits	Title/Form of address
Magistrates Court	Lay magistrates (usually 3) or a sole District Judge. Lay magistrates are assisted by the clerk to the justice to advise them on law, practice and procedure.	Sir/Madam, Your Worships, Mr/Madam Chairman.
County Courts	Circuit Judges/Deputy Circuit Judges, District Judges/Deputy District Judges. Who sits depends on value and/or complexity of case. A District Judge (a junior appointment) is appointed by the Lord Chancellor and must have a seven-year general qualification, for example as a solicitor or barrister (s.71 Courts and Legal Services Act 1990).	Circuit Judges: His/Her Honour, Judge Smith, Your Honour. District Judges: Judge Smith, Sir/Madam.
Crown Court	Depends on the gravity and/or nature of work: High Court Judge or Circuit Judge OR Recorder (part-time appointment, for example solicitor or barrister of 10 years' standing (s.71Courts and Legal Services Act 1990)). Magistrates may sit with judge on appeals AND jury for trial.	Depends on the status of the judge. A High Court Judge is addressed as Your Lordship/Your Ladyship.
High Court	One High Court Judge (called a puisne judge) usually sits. If necessary, a Circuit Judge, senior QC, Lord Justice, or a retired Judge may sit instead.	Mr/Mrs Justice Smith, Your Lordship/Your Ladyship.
Court of Appeal	Three, sometimes two Lord Justices of Appeal sit. The following can also sit: The Lord Chief Justice The Master of the Rolls High Court Judges as requested The Lord Chancellor and Vice-Chancellor The President of the Family Division Retired Lord Justices of Appeal.	Lord/Lady Justice Smith, Your Lordship/Your Ladyship.
House of Lords	Three to seven (but usually five) Lords of Appeal in Ordinary (the 'Law Lords'). The following can also sit: The Lord Chancellor Peers who hold (or have held) high judicial office.	Lord Smith of [Weesex], Your Lordship/Your Ladyship, My Lord/My Lady.
Coroners Court	A coroner has to have been qualified as a solicitor, barrister or medical practitioner for a minimum of five years. In reality, experience of nearer 20 years will be required. The approval of the Secretary of State is required for the appointment of any person as coroner.	Sir/Madam.

(Continued)

Scottish Courts

Court	Who sits	Title/Form of address
District Court	Lay Justice of the Peace (assisted by a legally qualified clerk to advise them on law, practice and procedure).	Sir/Madam.
Sheriff Court	Sheriff.	Sheriff Smith, My Lord/My Lady, Your Lordship/Your Ladyship.
Court of Session	Senator of the College of Justice (Lord Ordinary).	Lord/Lady Smith, My Lord/My Lady, Your Lordship/Your Ladyship.
High Court	Lord Commissioner of Justiciary.	Lord/Lady Smith, My Lord/My Lady, Your Lordship/Your Ladyship.
Court of Appeal (civil)	Three Senators of the College of Justice.	Lord/Lady Smith, My Lord/My Lady, Your Lordship/Your Ladyship.
Court of Appeal (criminal)	Three Lord Commissioners of Justiciary.	
House of Lords	Three to seven (but usually five) Lords of Appeal in Ordinary (the 'Law Lords'). The following can also sit: The Lord ChancellorPeers who hold (or have held) high judicial office.	Lord Smith of Perthshire, My Lord/My Lady, Your Lordship/Your Ladyship.
Fatal Accident Inquiry	Sheriff.	Sheriff Smith, My Lord/My Lady, Your Lordship/Your Ladyship.

in circumstances where the therapist may be acutely aware of the grief of any relatives who are present, or in some instances feeling under pressure to justify the way the work has been managed. A complicating factor is the ethical concern about what is appropriate to disclose about a client following his or her death. Most therapists find appearing in the coroner's court a professionally challenging experience. Prior knowledge and careful preparation is widely thought to be the best way of coping with the experience.

What are the functions of the coroner's courts?

The coroner is required to hold an inquest following the discovery of a body within the court's district, where there is reasonable cause to suspect that the deceased:

- Has died a violent or an unnatural death.
- Has died a sudden death of which the cause is unknown; or
- Has died in prison or in such a place or in such circumstances as to require an inquest under any other legislation.

It follows, therefore, that the primary function of the coroner's court is to establish the identity of the deceased and to determine the cause of death. An inquest is a formal court hearing, which is held to inquire into the circumstances and the cause of sudden or unnatural deaths, as long as they are not the subject of current criminal proceedings. An inquest is also held whenever a person dies in prison and into most deaths in police custody.

Conclusions relating to why a death occurred and how something similar can be prevented from happening again are also reached. As a result, inquiries are inquisitorial and investigative rather than adversarial (Pattenden, 2003: 530). Coroners are generally qualified solicitors and in some cases doctors.

Coroners are required to establish:

- Who died?
- How they died?
- When and where the death occurred?

This is not a trial and the coroner is not required to attribute blame for an individual's death. An inquest is opened to record that a death has occurred and to identify the deceased. It is usually adjourned until any police inquiries and the coroner's investigations are completed, when the full inquest may be resumed.

If an individual has been charged with homicide, the inquest on the victim must be adjourned and it is at the discretion of the coroner whether or not to resume until after the trial. If the inquest is resumed, its findings must be consistent with the outcome of the trial.

Inquest before a jury and the potential verdicts of an inquest

The vast majority of inquests are now heard by the coroner sitting alone. However, there are a number of instances where an inquest should be heard before a jury (s.8 (3) Coroners Act 1988):

- A death within a prison whatever the cause of death.
- The death occurring while the deceased was in police custody, or resulting from an injury caused by a police officer in the purported execution of his duty.
- Death caused by an accident, poisoning or disease, notice of which must be given to a government department or inspector.
- If a death occurred in circumstances which might cause another fatality, should the circumstances reoccur, then there must be a jury.

Where there is a jury, it is the jury and not the coroner, which makes the final decision about the legal cause of death. Where a case involves the possibility of suicide, the hearing will usually be heard by a coroner sitting alone. The different verdicts are listed below:

- Natural causes.
- Industrial disease.
- Dependence on drugs/non-dependent abuse of drugs.
- From want of attention at birth.
- Killed himself/herself while the balance of his/her mind was disturbed (suicide).
- Died as a result of an attempted/self-induced abortion.
- Accident/misadventure.
- Killed lawfully, for example, self-defence.
- Killed unlawfully, without reference to the culprit.
- Open verdict, where the evidence does not point to how the death arose.

Who decides which witnesses to call?

During an inquest, coroners have considerable powers to call upon any witnesses whom they consider to have relevant information relating to the inquiry and to determine how witnesses are questioned. There are great variations in practice between coroners in how they run their courts in these respects, but they share a general commitment to ensuring that a fair and balanced account of the death is obtained. It is also possible to request a list of the witnesses that are to be called, with a brief summary of their place in the chain of evidence. If an individual believes that someone who can provide relevant information about the death is not going to be called, then they can ask the coroner to call that person. Coroners can refuse, but could be challenged later for failing to make sufficient inquiry into the circumstances of a death. Following the death of their client, it is common practice for the therapist to be called to give evidence as a witness, especially where there is the possibility that the client committed suicide. The therapist must be informed of the date, time and place of the inquest.

Can therapists refuse to attend coroners court as a witness?

The coroner has the authority to compel witnesses to attend. Where a person is summoned to give evidence at an inquest, and does not appear after being openly called three times, or where they appear in response to the summons but refuse without a lawful excuse to answer questions, the coroner is allowed to impose a fine of no more than £400 on that individual (section 10 (2) Coroners Act 1988). This authority is in addition to the coroner's powers to compel a person to appear and give evidence in an inquest and to punish an individual for contempt of court in not appearing and giving evidence (section 10 (3) Coroners Act 1988). The summons must be delivered to the witness personally. This is usually undertaken by a police officer, who then reports to the coroner that the summons has been served.

Who can ask a witness questions in coroners court?

The usual reason for requiring therapists to appear as witnesses is to establish the cause of death. In particular, where the deceased is suspected of committing suicide, the court is interested in learning about the mental state and mood of the deceased and whether they had expressed any intention to end their life.

When called, the therapist needs to decide how much they are willing to say in open court. The coroner will usually start questioning the therapist to elicit the relevant facts and other *properly interested persons* are entitled to ask additional relevant questions of any witnesses called to give evidence. A solicitor or barrister may ask the therapist questions on behalf of these persons. The questions must be pertinent to the purpose of the inquest. The coroner can disallow any question that he or she considers to be irrelevant or improper. It is not the function of a coroner's inquest to provide opportunities to gather evidence for any other criminal or civil proceedings (Dorries, 1999: 159).

Therapists should be aware that the deceased's family may wish to ask some questions. This is one of the main sources of concern for therapists. Depending on the nature of the questions posed, the therapist may feel that they are choosing between protecting the confidentiality of the deceased and responding to questions arising from the acute grief of the surviving relatives. In some instances the therapist may feel that the questions are hostile with a view to seeking information on the way the therapist had worked with the client. It is generally accepted among therapists that client confidentiality continues beyond the client's death and this is often the reason why there is reluctance to attend the inquest for the purpose of giving evidence.

However, interested persons who want to ask questions are not permitted to embark on a 'fishing expedition' in order to coax out any details of what might have been said in the counselling sessions. The coroner will provide a clear explanation about what types of questions are permitted. For example, the coroner will usually be concerned to restrict questions that relate to the cause of death rather than allow the family to seek information about the client's views of the family or aspects of the client's life about which they had previously been unaware. When therapists are particularly concerned over issues of confidentiality, they are well advised to discuss these concerns with a coroner or one of the coroners' officers, before the inquest takes place. Most coroners are approachable and familiar with the dilemmas experienced by conscientious professionals. However, therapists need to always bear in mind that the law requires them to answer all relevant questions subject only to the right of refusal set out in Rule 22 Coroners Court Rules 1984; namely that no witness at an inquest shall be obliged to answer any question tending to incriminate themselves. Therefore, nobody can refuse to answer a relevant question on the grounds that it would be a breach of confidentiality.

The coroner is not only usually the first person to ask questions of any witness but also directs the way other interested parties may question that witness. The questions which individuals are permitted to ask must be considered by the coroner to be 'relevant' and 'proper' and will advise witnesses that they do not have to reply to questions if the answers may incriminate them (Victims Voice, 2002: 10). The conclusion reached by the coroner (or the jury if there is one) should be based solely on the evidence given at the inquest.

Persons with a 'proper interest' who are entitled to ask questions include:

- Parent, child, spouse, or legal personal representative of the deceased.
- The person who may have a responsibility for the death.
- A beneficiary from an insurance policy relating to the deceased.
- Representatives of any relevant insurance company.
- Representative from a relevant trade union.
- Certain inspectors or representatives of enforcing authorities or persons appointed by a government department.
- The police.
- Any other person the coroner considers to have a legitimate interest for the purposes of the inquest.

As all inquests must be held in public, a member of the press is usually present, although they do not always report the case.

In Scotland, sudden deaths are investigated by means of fatal accident inquiries, which are regulated by the Fatal Accidents and Sudden Deaths Inquiry (Scotland) Act 1976. A fatal accident inquiry (FAI) must be held where the deceased apparently died as a result of an accident sustained at work, or where the death occurred when the individual was in legal custody. The Lord Advocate may also order a FAI where, for example, the death was sudden, suspicious or unexplained, or where it occurred in circumstances such as to give rise to serious public concern. The case is investigated by the local procurator fiscal (who is also in charge of investigating crimes), who has the power to compel any relevant witnesses to attend to provide a 'precognition' (statement) in relation to the death. It is an offence to fail to attend. The fiscal also has powers to seek an order to cite witnesses to attend the FAI itself. Again, failure to attend is an offence.

The FAI is heard by a sheriff and there is no jury. At the FAI, it is the duty of the procurator fiscal to adduce all evidence relative to the circumstances of the death. In addition to the procurator fiscal other parties are entitled to attend the FAI and adduce evidence. This includes the spouse and or a close relative of the deceased and, if the deceased died as the result of an accident at work, the employer of the deceased and perhaps a health and safety inspector. In addition, any other person whom the sheriff is satisfied has a sufficient interest in the inquiry may seek to lead evidence.

At the end of the FAI, the sheriff makes a finding which will deal with issues such as:

- Where and when the death took place.
- The cause of death.
- Any accident resulting in it.
- Any reasonable precautions whereby the death might have been avoided.

Proposals to change the coroner's system

Some changes are proposed to the coroner's system in England which therapists need to bear in mind:

- Instead of being appointed by the local authority, coroners will be employed by a national body.
- Juries will only be called on cases involving the death of someone compulsorily in the care of the state, or where the agents of the state may have caused the death.
- There will no longer be a right to refuse to answer questions which might lead to self-incrimination. Instead, a witness will be required to answer all questions in return for an undertaking that the testimony will not be used against the witness in any criminal trial. This will increase the effectiveness of the inquest as an inquiry into the facts.
- Deaths by suicide will be handled differently and will not routinely include a public inquest. The word 'suicide' will in future be avoided. Such deaths will be classified as 'death from a deliberate act of self-harm or injury.'

Conclusion

Being a witness is a serious responsibility. It requires careful preparation and good communication skills, often under the challenging circumstances of cross-examination. Witnesses are not normally allowed legal representation. Professional witnesses are not usually offered legal advice beforehand unless they actively seek it. This often means that they are left giving evidence without any awareness of the rules. Expert witnesses should normally have sought some prior training. Witnesses of fact are less likely to have received or sought any training unless their professional role involves court work. Even for people used to court work, being a witness can be a demanding experience. There are particular hazards when presenting evidence as a therapist. These are considered in Chapters 6 and 7 concerning child and adult witnesses.

In Scotland, the witness citation is in a different form to the one shown earlier. It will advise you of the name of the case and the date and time when you are required to attend court. If, after receiving a citation, you fail to attend court at the time and on the date stipulated, a warrant may be issued for your arrest.

5 Payment of Expenses and Fees

You are likely to incur expenses as a result of your involvement with the legal process. Practical things like how much to charge for expert witness services and how to claim these expenses are addressed in this short chapter. The relevant information and procedures relating to this are provided below.

Witness of fact

Expenses can be claimed from the party or party's solicitor who asks you to be a witness. These include:

- Costs of travelling to and from court.
- Cost of overnight accommodation if necessary.
- A reasonable amount to compensate you for any wages or income you may lose when you go to court.

If called as a witness on behalf of the defence, the court will give you a claim form and explain what expenses and allowances can be claimed. These will be paid within 5 working days from when the court receives a claim.

If you are called as a prosecution witness, you must get your claim form from the Crown Prosecution Service representative, who will explain to you which expenses can be claimed.

Expert witness

The best expert witness in most cases is likely to be the one who has practical experience of the area in which they are giving evidence, rather than the 'professional' expert witness – one who acts as an expert witness for a living. As a result, only therapists who possess a high level of competency and experience in their area of work are likely to be allowed to charge expert witness fees.

Time spent on preparing an expert report can also be charged. There is no fixed amount for preparing an expert report. It is for you to decide how much your time is worth. A contract for services should be drawn up prior to commencing any work and the amount and when it will be paid should also be agreed with the party (or party's solicitor).

Detailed guidelines relating to instructing expert witnesses and payment of expenses and fees can be found in *Instructing Expert Witnesses: Guidelines for*

Solicitors. The information that follows is a brief outline of what therapists will need to know.

Terms of the contract should be agreed with the expert witness, and these should include:

- The basis of the expert's charges, for example the daily or hourly rates of the experts to be engaged and an estimate of the time likely to be required or alternatively an agreed reasonable fee for the services.
- Travel expenses.
- Likely expenses or disbursements.
- Rates for attendance at court.
- Time taken to produce an expert witness report.
- Contingency provision for payment in the event of late notice of cancellation of a court hearing.

Agreed fees should be paid within the timescale specified by the expert's terms of business agreed by the solicitor. He or she is personally responsible for paying the proper costs of any professional agent or other person whom they instruct on behalf of their client, whether or not they receive payment by their client. This is the case, unless:

- There is an agreement to the contrary, for example, where the client has agreed to pay the expert directly.
- The witness has declined an invitation to give evidence and has to be summoned.
- The solicitor has expressly disclaimed to the expert personal responsibility for payment of costs and fees.

Where attendance at court is required:

- In civil cases, solicitors are responsible for paying the reasonable expenses of the expert witness in attending court and giving evidence.
- In criminal cases, the expenses of the expert witness in travelling to and from court, the attendance fee and other expenses are paid by the court.

In Scotland the court is never responsible for the fees or expenses of a witness.

In *criminal* cases, a witness can claim their expenses and any fees from the prosecution service. However, the amount of any expert fee is likely to be limited. If appearing for the defence, any expenses and fees should be claimed from the accused's solicitor.

In *civil* proceedings, the therapist giving evidence of fact is entitled to claim his expenses of attending court from the party who is calling him as a witness. If the therapist is giving expert evidence or writing a report, he or she is entitled to charge whatever fees or expenses that have been agreed with the party instructing them.

Part Two

Working with clients involved in the law

6
Counselling Child Witnesses

Therapists working with child victims and witnesses of crime have an increasingly difficult job on their hands. As well as coping with the emotional impact of their ordeal at the hands of their perpetrator, victims also frequently have to deal with the traumatic experience of coming into contact with law enforcement agencies and taking legal action against their offender. The latter can be described as secondary victimisation at the hands of the legal system. Even where therapists attempt to help clients in addressing and resolving these problems, their efforts are hampered by the constraints of legal rules relating to the contamination of evidence (Williams, 2002: 116). Furthermore, where a trial is still ongoing, the therapist is sometimes drawn into the proceedings through requests for notes, attendance at court as a witness and reports. These difficulties and ways to cope with these situations are discussed in this chapter.

This chapter considers three areas which therapists need to consider when counselling child victims and witnesses of crime:

- Secondary traumatisation and the role of therapy.
- Pre-trial therapy and the risk of contaminating evidence.
- Involvement of therapists in the legal process.

Secondary victimisation and the role of therapy

Knowing the ways in which secondary victimisation can occur, as a result of lawful intervention, will enable therapists to be aware of some of the issues that may have affected a client before the counselling process begins.

Involvement with the justice system in prosecuting the offender and bringing them to trial can often lead them to view the legal processes as less about meeting their individual needs and more about attributing blame and securing convictions. For example, although the police may be increasingly sympathetic to the needs of victims and witnesses, their agenda is an investigative one and witnesses are essentially a means to an end (Williams, 2002: 106). Interviewing by police can be stressful and tiring for children. Where a child has been a victim of physical or sexual abuse, he or she may have endured a physical examination, often an intimate medical examination and a video interview conducted by police and social services within a very short space of time. In such cases therapists need to be particularly sensitive.

The following are just some of the examples which child victims and witnesses have experienced.

- The judicial process may reinforce a sense of being powerless and abused which was experienced during the original crime. For example, trials are often delayed and re-scheduled, unpredictably and without satisfactory explanation, causing additional stress. The trial can occur months or even years after the crime took place and may act as an unwanted and untimely reminder of the original event.
- The process of having their evidence tested through cross-examination can make the witness feel as if they are on trial and that their evidence is in doubt. This can lead to significant distress. In an evaluation of Witness Service Support for child witnesses, 62% of the sample of children giving evidence claimed that they were worried about giving evidence.
- If the crime happens to be reported in the media, it could trigger various traumatic symptoms as the child is confronted with reminders of the crime in an uncontrolled and unwanted way. If details of the report do not fit in with their recollection, this may lead to confusion and further distress and, if personal details are misreported the victim may become very angry. Furthermore, the trial may re-ignite media interest despite the length of time which may have lapsed since the crime, and details about the background of the perpetrator and victim may be made public.

It may be useful for children and young people to talk through their frustration with the 'legal system'. Expressing their anger and addressing these frustrations may help them to understand the reasons for undergoing the myriad of procedures relating to a prosecution. Specifically, clients who will be giving evidence in court may benefit from the opportunity to talk through their concerns about the process. Therapists can also refer clients to Victim Support, which provides a Witness Service offering independent information and support to victims, witnesses and their families through child liaison workers, including information for children and parents or guardians about giving evidence. They can also arrange a pre-trial visit to the court to allow children to familiarise themselves with the environment.

Very often the problems following a traumatic experience are the result of victims and witnesses being unable to create a coherent narrative, i.e. to construct a story that makes sense. Giving evidence may provide structure and encouragement to tell the story that may otherwise be too frightening to tell. A successful trial and the act of giving evidence can be of enormous therapeutic benefit to the child witness. For example, by publicly endorsing the truth of the child's account, by emphasising that the child is not in any sense culpable and by squarely placing the burden of guilt on the offender, the child's mental health can be restored (Morgan and Zedner, 1992: 115). It can also help to restore belief in the meaningfulness and safety of the world and in repairing the child's sense of control, which is often shattered or at least dented by the crime. Prosecutions can therefore form part of the healing process.

However, most child witnesses do not expect to find the experience of giving evidence as being therapeutic. Standing up in court and re-telling the story can be a daunting prospect and the growing involvement of children in criminal proceedings has led to a number of changes in the law. Changes are taking place to reflect:

- That children suffer additional stress in taking part in court proceedings.
- That such stress may affect the way they give evidence.
- That there is nevertheless a need to bring to justice people who offend against children. (Ball et al., 1995: 83–86)

Special measures are available for children under the age of 17 and those alleged to be the victims of a sexual offence, to help make the process of giving evidence less traumatic. These child-friendly arrangements illustrate how the legal system is becoming more sensitive to the needs of victims. The measures include:

- Screens – preventing witnesses from being able to see the defendant.
- Evidence by witnesses can be given by means of a live TV link.
- Clearing the public gallery of the courtroom so that evidence can be given in private.
- Court officials removing wigs and gowns in court.
- Video-recorded cross-examination of the witness to be shown at trial instead of the witness being cross-examined live at trial.
- To enable an intermediary, for example an interpreter, to help a witness communicate with legal representatives in the case and the court.
- To be provided with such aids to communication as the court considers appropriate, with a view to enabling questions or answers to be communicated to or by the witness. (Chapter I of Part II ss 23–30, Youth Justice and Criminal Evidence Act 1999; Vulnerable Witnesses (Scotland) Act 2004)

These changes illustrate that steps are taking place to address the needs of child victims and witnesses, and lessen the impact of secondary victimisation at the hands of the criminal justice system. Having an awareness of these changes will assist therapists in dealing with their clients more effectively. It will help the therapist to be sensitive to any issues that may present themselves at any stage of the counselling process and address them by making the child aware of the safeguards that are in place and/or referring them to the appropriate service to help them with their concerns.

Pre-trial therapy and the risk of contaminating evidence

Child witnesses have sometimes been denied access to therapy if a prosecution is pending. Some therapists have avoided such work because of fears that their notes may be subject to a court order, or that they themselves may end up having to give evidence in court about their work with the child. There is a view that such work is ineffective prior to the trial and that any progress made would be 'undone' by the legal proceedings. Some organisations have even adopted a policy of not offering therapeutic treatment to child witnesses prior to the trial.

However, a more common and frequent reason is that therapists are anxious not to prejudice the evidence the victim will be giving. Discussions about the content of evidence prior to a trial may give rise to questions about the validity of the victim's evidence. This is not a psychological question about the reliability of the child's memory, but a legal question about the perceived credibility of the evidence. For example:

- In giving numerous accounts in therapy of what happened, discrepancies may appear, which, if brought to the attention of the court, would undermine the perceived validity of the evidence.
- Through the therapeutic discussion, the victim may remember more details than they gave in their original statement. If this additional information is brought up in court under cross-examination, the witness may be open to the accusation that they have fabricated the details since their initial statement, thus undermining the validity of their evidence.
- One of the specific aims of therapy is to make the event less distressing to the victim enabling them to tell the story with less visible signs of distress. This will lessen the impact on a jury, which may lead the court to disbelieve the account because the victim, having put the event behind them, appears to be coping *too* well. (Spencer, 1992: 113–129)
- By telling the story in therapy, in advance of the trial, the child or young person may realise that there are various gaps in their account, and wish to fill these in before actually giving evidence.

Any one of these considerations could ultimately undermine the validity of evidence in the eyes of the court and, thereby, lead to the prosecution failing. This in turn might then have significant negative effects upon the child, especially if they are made aware of the reasons for the prosecution failing. Furthermore, if such a detrimental effect is foreseeable by therapists, then he or she could be considered to be negligent. On the other hand children may be denied effective treatment at a time when it is needed. Waiting until after the trial may lead to a decline in the child's mental health and make the problems more difficult to treat when therapy is finally offered.

The decision to commence therapy therefore needs to be taken after careful consideration. The Guidance on 'Provision of Therapy for Child Witnesses Prior to a Criminal Trial' was issued jointly by the Home Office, the Crown Prosecution Service (CPS), and the Department of Health (Home Office et al., 2001). It was a response to the dilemmas discussed above and concerns over the length of time that child victims were waiting before gaining access to counselling. It should therefore carry substantial weight with the police, solicitors and therapists. It is a means of overcoming the perceived conflict between providing pre-trial therapy to assist children and tainting the evidence, and is useful for therapists as it sets out a framework for good practice, while trying to ensure that standards of evidence required by the courts are met. Anyone who is providing therapy to a child who may have to give evidence should have a copy of this Guidance. The following section summarises the key points arising out of the Guidance and may help therapists to reach a decision, which is in the best interests of the child or young person concerned.

Guidelines on the use of therapy

All those working with children before a criminal trial need to be aware of the possible impact of their work upon subsequent evidence in the trial. Some types of therapeutic work are more likely to be seen as prejudicial and thereby undermine the perception of a child's credibility and reliability or to influence a child's memory of an event or the account they give (Home Office et al., 2001: para 5.2).

If therapists are in doubt about the likely effect of a particular type of therapy on the evidence they can contact the CPS for advice. The judge may also be consulted if the criminal case is at an advanced stage. Some form of discussion with the CPS is likely to be crucial and permission for such discussions should be sought from the client. Therapists need to make it clear to clients that it is simply the process of therapy, and not the content of counselling sessions, that will be discussed. Generally, clients will allow such a discussion once they are aware of the possible impact of therapy on the prosecution's case.

Decision making

The CPS can comment on the impact of the therapy on the trial, but not on the therapeutic needs of the child or young person. This is the role of the therapist. The Guidance explicitly states that those involved in the prosecution have no authority to prevent a child from receiving therapy (para 6.1). Decisions about therapy involve balancing various factors to decide the best interests of the child. If there is a demonstrable need for the provision of therapy and it is possible that the therapy will prejudice the criminal proceedings, consideration may need to be given to abandoning those proceedings in the interests of the child's well-being (para 4.5). The therapist would then need to consider the consequences of abandoning the proceedings on the mental health of the child.

The different types of therapeutic work and their potential threat to evidence is depicted in Figure 6.1.

Figure 6.1   Therapeutic work and potential threat to evidence

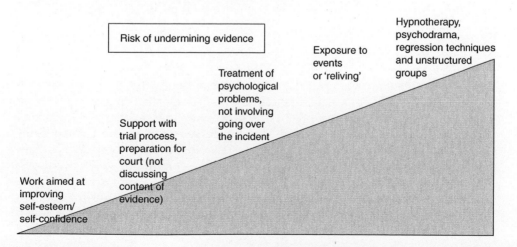

It is evident that the higher up the spectrum you go the more chance there is of evidence being undermined. Therapeutic work involving hypnotherapy and/or psychodrama is more likely to be viewed as undermining the perception of a child's credibility and reliability. A good line of practice may be to compromise, so that certain types of therapy are provided before the trial, while delaying other types until after the trial. For example, limited therapy, which does not involve going over the crime and focuses on building the client's self-confidence, could be used before the trial, leaving other more 'penetrative' forms of therapy until the trial has ceased.

Whatever conclusion therapists come to with regard to providing therapy, there is a need to ensure that consultation with the relevant professionals takes place. These include child protection professionals that may be involved and the CPS. In all cases, the course of action that is in the child's best interests should be taken.

The Scottish Executive has also issued guidance for therapists in Scotland, in the form of its publications 'Interviewing Child Witnesses in Scotland' (2003) and 'Code of Practice to Facilitate the Provision of Therapeutic Support to Child Witnesses in Court Proceedings' (2005). Both of these publications are available on the Scottish Executive website at www.scotland.gov.uk. The latter publication advises that, if a therapist is concerned that any counselling provided might contaminate the child witness's evidence, then advice can be sought in that regard from the Procurator Fiscal. As above, however, the decision as to whether or not a child should receive counselling is a matter for the child, his or her guardian/s and the therapist involved.

Involvement of therapists in the legal process

How confidential is therapy prior to a trial?

If, having carefully considered the issues above, the decision is made to go ahead with therapy, then issues surrounding the confidential nature of the therapy need to be addressed by the therapist. As the client's therapist, you may be asked to complete a report or give evidence concerning the impact of the crime on the child or young person. This might be as part of a criminal prosecution, or as part of a compensation claim.

Considerations before therapy is started

Because confidentiality is crucial to building trust with the child, a breach of confidentiality could potentially undermine and destroy any benefits gained from the therapeutic work. It is best practice for such issues to be explicitly discussed at the outset of therapy so that the child or young person and their carers are not surprised by such procedures. It should be possible to discuss under what circumstances the therapist might be required to disclose information, whilst reassuring the client that aspects of therapy that have no material relevance to criminal proceedings will not be disclosed. For example, although a request for information can be made, those involved with the prosecution (i.e. the police, the prosecutor, the defence and the court) do not have the right of access to information relating to therapy, as a matter of course. The Guidance is clear that requests for information should not be used by the defence or prosecution to satisfy their curiosity (Home Office et al., 2001: para 3.10).

Disclosure after therapy has commenced

If during the course of the counselling process, disclosure of information is requested, then you should consider such requests together with the child or young person and, where appropriate, whoever has parental responsibility. More practically, therapists should seek to obtain appropriate legal advice. If, having consulted with the client and taken appropriate legal advice, the therapist declines the request, those requesting the information may apply to the court for a court order to obtain the material. Disclosure can be compelled if there are real grounds for believing that there is relevant material, which could affect the outcome of the case. The therapist can opt to oppose this application and this can lead to a hearing at which both the applicant and the therapist are represented, where the court will decide whether or not to issue a witness summons requiring the disclosure of the material. More information on court orders is given in Chapter 2. Because of the recognition that maintaining the child's trust is central to the provision of therapy, it will usually only be appropriate to breach confidentiality in compliance with a court order (para 3.15).

Having established the confidential nature of the therapy or counselling, it may take careful explanation and negotiation with the child or young person to explain that he or she is reporting to the court based on what they have been told 'in confidence'. Even if the young person wishes the therapist to do so, there may be some work required after the trial to re-establish the client's understanding of confidentiality.

Assisting the court to understand the impact of the crime on the child

Therapists may be called on behalf of the prosecution, in their capacity as a professional witness to give their professional opinion relating to the impact of a crime on the child. However, therapists are advised against this. It is tempting to think that a therapist, who has been working closely with their client, can provide some helpful information to the court. This can lead to complications:

- The court may rightly question the impartiality of a therapist who has developed a therapeutic alliance with a client which may undermine the credibility of the evidence.
- The court may want answers to questions that were not covered within the counselling sessions, so the practitioner has to decide how far, if at all, to stray from their therapeutic agenda in order to meet the needs of the court, which may or may not be in the client's best interests. For example, the court may wish to know whether the child suffered from post-traumatic stress disorder immediately after the crime or at any time since. If this was not part of the therapist's initial assessment then he or she may not be able to answer the question.

An important point to make here is that to assess the impact of a crime on a child, an assessment by an expert witness who is wholly objective and impartial is required and therapists should make this clear to the person making the request. This might be an assessment undertaken by a specialist, perhaps a clinical psychologist used to undertaking these assessments for courts. It may well be that therapists have some useful information that could assist a court in awarding damages and which might be in the client's best interests. In such cases they could suggest writing a report instead, detailing the relevant information.

Chapter summary

- Therapists need to be aware of the problems relating to providing therapy to child victims and witnesses.
- Secondary victimisation experienced by coming into contact with the criminal justice system need to be addressed as well as the primary victimisation suffered at the hands of the perpetrator. Having an awareness of the measures designed to make the criminal justice more child-friendly will assist therapists to provide the best service for their clients.
- The risks relating to pre-trial therapy need to be considered carefully. The decision to commence therapy in cases where children will be required to give evidence in court should be reached after consultation with the relevant professionals and in light of the child's best interests.
- As a result of counselling child witnesses, therapists may be drawn into the legal proceedings, in one form or another. Therapists are advised to discuss this with their clients and their carers before commencing therapy. It is also wise to prevent direct involvement by making solicitors aware of the limits of your professional competence.

Counselling Adult Victims and Witnesses

This chapter provides an overview of the issues relating to counselling victims of crime or civil wrongs (sometimes referred to by lawyers as torts) and adults who require psychological or personal support in order to appear as witnesses in court. The challenges of offering therapy to people in these circumstances are changed by their involvement with the formal systems of justice. A therapist who is working with an ordinary adult client will usually place a high priority on the well-being of that client and the client's autonomy. This is the usual professional ethic. As soon as a client becomes a witness in court proceedings they are exposing themselves to an environment with different ethical priorities. The ethic of justice is concerned with achieving fairness between all the parties to a case over and above the short-term well-being of any of the parties. This makes courts a particularly challenging environment for any adult to appear if they are experiencing a sense of vulnerability due to the circumstances that have caused them to appear before the court or because of some pre-existing vulnerability. Although courts try to be increasingly sensitive to the needs of adults appearing in front of them, especially as witnesses or the victims of someone else's actions, they are not therapeutic organisations. This means that therapists supporting adult witnesses have to be mindful of the needs of justice and avoiding compromising court proceedings by invalidating witness evidence while maximising the appropriate support for the client. Once the court appearance is completed the normal therapeutic priorities can prevail.

The victims of crime and civil wrongs have usually not only suffered because of the harm done to them but also suffer constraints on the services available to them until the completion of the trial. This chapter opens by considering general issues relating to supporting victims who are involved in court proceedings. As by no means all victims choose to report offences against them or to sue for damages, the next section considers the issue of supporting victims who have chosen not to participate in legal proceedings or have been deprived of the opportunity of a court case, perhaps due to lack of evidence. The final group of adults involved in court proceedings considered in this chapter are intimidated witnesses and those with pre-existing vulnerabilities. This last group may include both independent witnesses as well as victims, in the sense that victims are witnesses to the offence against themselves.

Supporting victims involved in court proceedings

Public policy in the UK and internationally has tended to move towards recognising the needs of all witnesses in court proceedings over the last decade. Most courts have made provisions to answer general queries from witnesses who are not otherwise legally represented. In most criminal courts, there are witness support services. In addition, Victim Support is an independent body that provides services for victims of crime throughout the UK. Most of their services are provided by trained volunteers often from the area in which the person requiring support lives. These organisations and their workers have a great deal of specialised local knowledge.

Government has sought to address the needs of victims, initially by introducing and then revising the Victim's Charter in 1996 (Home Office, 2004). According to the Charter there are 27 standards of service that victims and their families can expect to receive from the Criminal Justice Agencies after a crime has been reported to the police. The government plans to replace this Charter by a statutory Victims Code of Practice in 2005–2006. In summary, victims can expect:

- A crime to be investigated and to receive information about what happens.
- The chance to explain how the crime has affected them and their interests to be taken into account.
- That, if you have to go to court as a witness, you will be treated with respect and sensitivity.
- To be offered emotional and practical support.
- Therapists are advised to discuss this with their clients, their carers and when appropriate their solicitors. The only way of avoiding going to court altogether is not to take on clients involved in litigation and even that cannot be guaranteed.

Support for witnesses in the civil courts is less developed, in part because there is generally less need for witnesses to appear in person. In most cases a sworn witness statement recorded in writing is sufficient. Witnesses who are troubled by the events associated with a traumatic civil case, for example, witnessing a serious industrial accident or a road traffic collision, are more exclusively dependent on therapists and their own social networks for support. For this reason this chapter will be primarily concerned with issues associated with criminal cases although many of the general principles are transferable to civil cases where a client is likely to be required to give evidence in person. In this case, advice should be sought through their lawyer or from the court if possible, before commencing therapy related to the incident being considered at court.

Although public policy has moved towards recognising the needs of victims of crime, there are still substantial constraints:

- Services are not universally available and may be in limited supply or insufficient to meet the level of demand. The use of resources released by the confiscation of proceeds of crime is making an impact. For example, substantial additional sums, about £4 million pounds, have been made available to enhance services for victims of sexual crimes in 2005.
- People living in deprived areas are more likely to be a victim of crime.
- People on low incomes are least likely to be adequately insured against loss and any hope of restoring personal effects are shattered.

- Loss from a low level of possessions represents a proportionately more significant harm than the same value of loss for someone with greater wealth.
- Most services tend to be concentrated on the victims and witnesses of crime rather than their families. However, family members can be troubled by the change in mood and behaviour of the person affected and may not understand the potential consequences of psychological trauma. Family members who are supportive may themselves become as vulnerable to secondary traumatisation as the professionals involved in working with the victims of traumatic events and may be less well linked into support networks. The development of family liaison services delivered by police officers to families affected by murder, kidnapping and other serious crime provides some help that often continues beyond legal proceedings. Similarly, some police forces have developed services to support families affected by fatal road accidents. These types of developments are in line with the growing appreciation of the cascade effect of trauma beyond the victim into their social networks. The United Nations Declaration of Basic Principles of Justice for Victims of Crime and Abuse of Power (1985) regards family members as secondary victims and directs attention to the effect that crime has on the whole family.

However, constraints on providing adequate therapy to victims and traumatised witnesses cannot be resolved by ensuring the provision of adequate resources alone. The biggest constraint arises from the legal system itself and the established practices of the courts. Criminal courts in Britain have tended to rely heavily on the oral evidence of witnesses. The truthfulness and accuracy of witness evidence is tested by cross-examination and ultimately a decision is made about the weight attached to the evidence that depends on the impression made by individual witnesses.

Risk to evidence

Avoiding the contamination of witness evidence is a high priority in the delivery of fair trials. Contamination can lead to false convictions as well as false acquittals. Discussions with witnesses prior to trials have led to both these outcomes. The courts have been particularly concerned about pre-trial discussions with witnesses that that have led to:

- Witnesses giving inconsistent accounts of events in their evidence.
- Fabrication of accounts of events, whether deliberate or inadvertent. For example, a witness may become aware of gaps or inconsistencies in evidence by comparing evidence with others. As a consequence, the witness may become more convinced, or convincing, about the evidence but nonetheless mistaken.

There are many types of pre-trial discussion that could lead to evidence being challenged either in the trial or at appeal. Informal contacts with friends and family can distort evidence and change someone's recollection. The operational debriefing of police officers where their evidence is later required for trial, for example, following a major public disorder incident, has been held to damage the integrity of the evidence given in court. Training witnesses to give evidence can also invalidate that evidence. For example, it is acceptable to train witnesses on fictional cases unrelated to the actual case in order to familiarise them with court procedure and communications skills but it is considered unacceptable to rehearse giving evidence for the actual case. Therapy is viewed by courts as only one of many forms of pre-trial discussion that can adversely affect a fair trial.

The main concern with regard to pre-trial discussions of any kind is the potential impact on the reliability of the evidence of the witnesses and the difficulty it creates in court in being able to determine the weight to be given to that evidence. Courts are as concerned about evidence being actually influenced as by the perception that it may have been influenced. Even a false suspicion of contaminated evidence can undermine confidence in the outcome of a trial. It is always in the defence's interest within an adversarial criminal trial to seek to discredit any evidence against a defendant and any ill-focused or poorly disciplined pre-trial counselling sessions are easy targets for allegations of 'coaching' with the effect of partially or wholly undermining the evidence. Therapists are a relatively easy target for these allegations. As soon as the defence knows that therapy has taken place they will realise that this is a potential area of weakness in the prosecution's case. They will also be aware that therapists have a collective reputation for being poor witnesses in the box. They are viewed as a wild card who can often be tempted into making comments that the defence can exploit.

Therapists who are untrained in giving evidence and the expectations of courts blunder blindly on the false assumption that their skills in the therapy room will protect them in the box. The reality is probably the opposite. Many therapists may have made better witnesses before they trained as therapists. Most therapy trainings increase sensitivity to the client's subjective experience, whether cognitive, emotional or interpersonal, and train the therapist to use their own subjectivity strategically to advance the therapeutic process. Therapy of all kinds validates subjectivity and each therapy has its preferred concepts and language to communicate its insights about healing subjective wounds. Taking an impartial and objective with a fixation on facts is exactly what most therapists have been trained away from. Yet, it is these very unwanted characteristics in a therapist that make a good witness. The best witnesses have an ability to communicate a fact as clearly and simply as possible, stripped of irrelevant detail and personal or professional opinion, especially when based on subjective experience. Therapeutic jargon should be avoided at all times. It may be quoted out of context later in the trial in ways that the witness had not intended. Alternatively, it may open up dangerous lines of questioning in cross-examination, firstly about the meaning of the term, and then its application to this client. The request for few specific examples opens up endless possibilities in cross-examination. It is often the therapist who wants to use their time in the box to impress with their therapeutic competence or the brilliance of a particular approach to therapy that is easiest prey in cross-examination. They are playing the wrong game to the wrong rules, rather like someone unknowingly playing 'Blind Man's Buff', a children's party game, in the middle of a closely fought rugby match. The outcome tends to be painful for the therapist and ultimately can be very damaging to the client's respect and trust, especially if his or her case is damaged, however

Table 7.1 Therapists as witnesses

What to do	Further guidance	What to avoid
Be impartial	Value fairness and justice between all parties to the case.	Avoid taking sides or acting as an advocate for one party.
Be objective	Concentrate on what your client did or said.	Exclude your subjective impressions or experiences.
Be factual	Focus on what happened and when.	Avoid speculation or therapeutic interpretations unless specifically asked. If asked, be cautious as witnesses of fact are not normally permitted to express opinions, whether personal or professional.
Be clear	Use everyday language in simple short sentences.	Avoid jargon and therapeutic technical terms.
Be relevant	Only disclose information that is asked for and that is relevant to the case. All other matters should remain confidential.	Don't try to give the full therapeutic process or be tempted to talk about the most interesting or professionally challenging aspects of the case.
Be prepared	Identify the key facts in advance. Think how you can communicate these if asked. Think of possible challenges. How will you answer suggestions that you *coached* the witness?	Don't neglect possible challenges to your evidence as witness. Think ahead and get advice before you are in the witness box.
Be willing to be boring	Focus on giving relevant factual information as clearly as possible.	Don't try to promote yourself as a brilliant therapist or to sell your approach to therapy.
Remain calm and considered	Listen to the words of questions rather than the manner in which they are put. Win respect by remaining calm under pressure.	Avoid being provoked.

unwittingly. It is salutary to remember that in most cases it is the client who has most at stake and who is most vulnerable if the therapist fails to be adequately prepared on how to give evidence as a witness or fails to act professionally and fairly to all parties in the case (see Table 7.1).

One of us, Tim Bond, has heard an experienced Crown Prosecution Officer, who is personally sympathetic to therapy, curse therapists as naïve witnesses for the defence. Some of the force of this comment was directed at their naïvety when called as witnesses to testify about the therapy undertaken. Following the practices suggested in Table 7.1 will go a long way to addressing this concern. Getting some advice and guidance, or even training, on how to communicate as a witness would be even better. The other area of concern is the therapist's management of therapeutic records, which is to be elaborated on in the next volume in this series.

From the moment the therapist knows that a client is likely to appear as a witness, it is good practice to keep brief factual notes of all contacts. These should include the date and time of the contact and a succinct statement about the content of the session, for example, 'confidence building', 'stress management', or 'relationship difficulties with partner'. The notes should also include brief records of any discussions with the authorities, typically the police or the Crown Prosecution Service (in Scotland, the Procurator Fiscal Service), about the possibility of providing therapy. The Guidelines state 'Careful recording is essential' (Home Office et al., 2001: section 6.5).

The way forward

Therapists working with witnesses and victims in criminal cases should work in the knowledge that they may be called to give evidence. Government guidance is unequivocal:

> It should be borne in mind that the professional concerned may themselves be called to court as witnesses in relation to any therapy undertaken prior to a criminal trial. (Home Office et al., 2001: section 3.5)

The police or Crown Prosecution Service or the Procurator Fiscal Service should be informed about any planned or ongoing therapy at the earliest possible stage, whenever possible before the therapy has commenced. The police, the prosecutor, the defence or the court may make requests for information from therapists at various stages in criminal cases. Where the prosecution is aware that therapy has taken place it must inform the defence.

The Home Office guidelines tend to assume that the knowledge that someone might be a witness precedes the start of therapy. However, this is not always the case. The counselling, psychotherapy or psychology may have already started before the possibility of giving evidence has arisen. A typical example would be:

> Mary has been receiving counselling because of lack of confidence partially arising from a very controlling and violent relationship with her partner. Partly as a result of the counselling, she realises that she does not have to put up with being so abused and decides to report her partner following the next beating or sexual assault.

Increasingly, these types of cases involving domestic violence are supported by forensic evidence obtained as near to the time of the event as possible. However, if the client's oral evidence is critical to the case, it is likely that the therapist will be called by the defence in an attempt to establish coaching, to discredit Mary's motives or her reliability as a witness. An experienced counsellor in this sort of work would most probably support Mary in making a statement to the police at the earliest possible opportunity and would avoid any discussion of the details of the attack until the statement has been taken and any evidence has been collected.

A more difficult situation to manage is where a client is receiving therapy and seems disinterested in prosecuting an offender but changes their mind as the therapy proceeds. Again, the therapist would be well advised to support the client in making the earliest possible report of the offence to the police. In such circumstances, there is likely to be limited forensic evidence and the decision whether to prosecute and the outcome of the trial may well depend on evidence given by the victim and the therapist. Particular weight is attached to first accounts of any offence, which is why this may be better recorded by the police than the therapist. A therapist who can demonstrate attentiveness to avoiding contaminating evidence and who uses methods unlikely to influence the clients recollection of an incident, is likely to be much better regarded as a witness. In the witness box, the therapist may come under a lot of pressure in cross-examination to:

- Provide evidence that that will undermine the reliability of the client.
- Demonstrate inconsistencies between what the client has said to the police and the therapist.
- Establish therapy has coached the client in how they gave their evidence and therefore contaminated that evidence or has surreptitiously influenced the client into inventing the allegations.

Witnesses of fact, such as the therapist, are not permitted into court until they are due to give their evidence. This is to prevent them hearing the evidence of other parties and to prevent the sort of contamination that can arise in pre-trial discussions.

Good practice in supporting witnesses and victims requires a therapist to be systematic and rigorous in how they approach working with these clients until the trial is over. In the process of researching this chapter, we consider that the current practice of most therapists is vulnerable to criticism in court because of lack of appreciation of the issues at stake for both the client and therapist. For any therapist working with clients who are likely to appear as witnesses, particularly if they are the victim, it is advisable to:

- Be familiar with the latest guidance concerning support for victims, particularly concerning providing therapy to adult witnesses. This type of information is readily available on the web and from government departments.
- Have established policies and practice with regard to record keeping. Careful maintenance of contemporaneous records, made as close in time to the event as possible, will greatly assist meeting legal responsibilities in these types of cases.
- These records should include any assessment processes and consultations with the authorities about whether it is appropriate to provide therapy and on what terms. See later for the assessment of intimidated or vulnerable adult witnesses.

- Establish a policy about how to respond to requests for information in relation to court cases. Government guidance may be helpful. 'Because of the recognition that maintaining trust is central to the provision of therapy, it will usually only be appropriate to breach confidentiality in compliance with a court order' (Home Office et al., 2001: section 3.14). There is also guidance on seeking legal advice about responding to witness summons and the procedure for disputing these if the therapist 'believes that the information should not be disclosed' (section 3.13)

Choice of therapeutic methods

Courts regard some approaches to therapy prior to the witness appearing in court as more problematic than others. Cognitive and behavioural techniques are viewed as less problematic in general. Interpretive psychodynamic psychotherapy is perceived as potentially problematic, even if 'carefully conducted' (Home Office et al., 2001: sections 6.3 and 10.3). Hypnotherapy, psychodrama, regression techniques and unstructured groups are viewed as interfering with the reliability of the evidence. As a general principle group therapy should not be offered.

Even when using an unproblematic therapeutic method the subject matter of the therapy should avoid recounting the events associated with the court case in great detail or any reenactment of those events. *Criminal cases are almost certain to fail because this type of therapeutic work* (section 11.12). Therapy directed towards reducing the distress about impending legal proceedings, relationship difficulties, or about associated emotional and behavioural disturbance that does not require rehearsal of abusive events is viewed as much less problematic.

Coping with uncertainty and delay

One of the major challenges in supporting victims and witnesses is the level of uncertainty and delay that may be involved in waiting for a case to be heard. There are no standard procedures following the initial reporting of a crime. Police procedures vary according to the circumstances including the availability of resources, although serious crimes will usually be a priority. Cases may be adjourned several times. In serious cases there may be bail hearings, not usually requiring either witnesses or victims to attend, some form of committal proceedings, which may require giving evidence, and the trial proper which will require giving evidence.

For witnesses this creates a potential emotional helter-skelter of anticipation and disappointment that is probably inadequately appreciated by professional lawyers. One of the ways therapists may overstep the mark of being appropriately supportive of their clients is becoming irritated with obvious distress that delays and uncertainty may be causing a client. There may be no easy meeting of professional minds here. Therapists are highly sensitised to the psychological harm caused by unpredictable and endlessly deferred justice and the way it erodes any justice to their client. In contrast, lawyers are more concerned with issues of evidence and judicial procedure in what are often immensely complex bureaucratic exercises in which feelings, including the lawyers' own, are secondary to procedure and argument.

One of the concerns of witnesses faced with delays of months and sometimes years, is whether they will remember their evidence. In actual practice, witnesses of fact are usually allowed to refresh their memory by reading their police statement before giving evidence. They are not normally allowed to take notes with them into the witness box. They may also be concerned about going into an unfamiliar court environment. The witness support service in most courts is well placed to respond to these concerns.

One of the costs of the substantial delay is to the family and social relationships of witnesses and victims. The witness has to wait, however frustrated, for the wheels of justice to turn, partners, family and friends do not and as a result may detach themselves from the whole process. This is perhaps the highest cost often borne in major criminal trials and it is largely invisible to the court and the public. Perhaps the most significant improvement in the current legal process would be to expedite the procedures. However, although there have been many honest attempts to do so these have been without success. The legal maxim 'justice delayed is justice denied' doesn't really capture the experience of many therapists. Justice delayed increases the number of innocent victims.

Research into the impact of homicide highlights that therapists need to be aware of the frustration and anger felt by those who were powerless within the Criminal Justice System (Harrison, 2000: 38). In particular, any delays can affect the grieving process, heightening hopelessness and despair. When this occurs, it can lead to a higher incidence of depression.

The life of witnesses and especially victims is distorted and stressed throughout the period of time prior to an important court case. The withholding of therapy connected with this experience is only part of the story. One of the things therapists can usually do is to help clients minimise the stress by finding coping strategies and to help them with the inevitable strains in close relationships. These activities can usually be undertaken without straying into matters of evidence concerning the forthcoming case. Full therapy can be offered on completion of the case, usually regardless of whether it goes to appeal. The ending of a case is a major event. Many clients have a process of major adjustment to accomplish whether or not the case has worked out in their favour or has been a source of major disappointment.

Victims of sexual offences

Victims of sexual offences are also particularly vulnerable in the legal process. Between 1996 and 1997 the numbers of women reporting rape increased by over 500%, yet convictions have remained almost static at 10%. Furthermore, 1 in 4 women suffer rape or attempted rape (Rape Crisis Federation, 2004, http://www.cambridgerapecrisis.org.uk/rcf-archive/statistics.htm). Victims of sexual offences and rape are particularly fearful about reporting the crime for fear of disbelief, and it is important for the therapist to not only be concerned and compassionate, but also to be non-judgemental, sensitive, and empathetic. Sometimes there are cultural and other inhibitions to reporting rape. To become known as a victim of rape, whether the victim is male or female, is to be permanently degraded and marginalised in some cultures and some communities. The distress and psychological disturbance of rape victims is compounded if their case is dropped, and this may lead to increased anxiety, feelings of guilt and self-blame and increasing psychological damage.

Supporting victims not involved in court proceedings

Some people decide not to pursue what on the face of it appear to be legitimate claims in the civil courts or justifiable prosecutions in the criminal courts. The reasons for this are varied. Some simply prefer to move on with their lives rather than to be locked into litigation for a protracted period. Some view walking away from damaging experiences as a more healthy response than prolonging their experiences in the form of litigation. Some simply do not have the opportunity to seek justice or redress because of lack of evidence, lack of resources, cultural inhibitions, or concern for dependent family members. Others worry about retaliation and intimidation.

One of the challenges both clients and therapists face is that if the client is unsure or subsequently changes their mind from avoiding court proceedings, their case may be weakened by the combination of delay and the possibility of having received therapy that would contaminate future appearances in court as a witness. For these reasons, if there is the prospect of legal redress it would be prudent to ensure that a client has given it careful consideration before getting involved with therapy, particularly therapy directly related to the harmful event. In some cases, it may be appropriate to encourage a client to seek legal advice from organisations such as the Citizens' Advice Bureau or a solicitor. Where the decision is personal rather than legal the therapist may suggest reviewing the basis of the decision to ensure that it is as secure as it could reasonably be expected to be. The reasons for making a decision about whether to take part in legal action are very varied. They may be explored by strategies as simple as listing the factors for and against becoming involved in litigation. Different therapists will have their preferred methods of doing this and for some this would be their normal way of starting work with a client.

The advantage to both client and therapist is that once this decision has been taken and secured as far as possible, they are better placed to know whether they can adopt a client-led agenda or whether they need to take a more self-denying approach to any matters relating to a potential court case in order to meet the guidelines for offering therapy to adult witnesses.

What happens if the crime is not reported?

Since its inception in 1985 the British Crime Survey has consistently shown substantial amounts of crime which are not recorded by the police (Shepherd, 1998). The reasons for this are complex and range from shame and fear of reprisals to apathy. Research carried out by Victim Support establishes that victims who do not report a crime are more likely to discuss their experiences with a member of a health-related profession than with the police. 'Healthcare workers' are highly likely to see victims of unreported crime as they seek help to overcome any physical and psychological trauma. For whatever reason, these victims are unable to relate their experiences to anyone else. Therapists and other healthcare workers are therefore best placed to ask direct questions (Victim Support, 2002). An awareness of the kind of crimes that are committed against individuals will enable therapists to be better prepared to assist victims seeking counselling.

If the crime is not reported it is unlikely that the victim will be known to Victim Support or any other agency unless they decide to approach a service directly. Since most referrals to Victim Support come through the police, those offences which are not reported or recorded will not normally trigger a referral. The under-reporting of crime is a cause for concern and is readily apparent when looking at the number of victims who are seen at hospital accident and emergency departments in comparison to the number of crimes that are unreported. Adequate services for this group of victims are rarely available, although psychological and social support is often just as important to their recovery. Some victims will go on to develop serious psychological problems such as flashbacks, sleep disruption, depression and post-traumatic stress disorder. At this point a swift and co-ordinated response from victim support agencies can make a real difference to the health and quality of the victim's life (Shepherd, 1997). In some cases the therapist may be best placed to provide this support.

Intimidated and vulnerable witnesses

Intimidated and vulnerable witnesses have gained substantial new rights in recent years in response to 'Speaking up for Justice' (Interdepartmental Working Group, 1998). This report not only expressed concern that witnesses were being unnecessarily and inappropriately denied therapy pending the outcome of criminal trials but it set out the basis on which therapy may be offered to all witnesses and specifically for those who are intimidated and vulnerable. In the subsequent guidance, 'the best interests of the vulnerable or intimidated witnesses are the paramount consideration in decisions about the provision of therapy before a criminal trial' (Home Office et al., 2001: section 4.4 and repeated in slightly different words in section 8.5). The principle that the best interests of the witness should take priority is further elaborated by other guidance, 'If the prosecutor advises that the proposed therapy may prejudice the criminal case, this should be taken into account (by a multidisciplinary meeting that includes the therapist) when deciding whether to agree to therapy. It may still be in the best interests of the witness to proceed with the therapy' (section 11.7).

The guidelines envisage a thorough assessment of the needs and wishes of vulnerable and intimidated witnesses. Both the assessment and the therapy should be undertaken by 'a trained professional person, with a recognised competence, such as a social worker, psychiatrist, psychologist, psychotherapist, nurse or other relevant qualified person' (section 8.7).

When assessing therapy, therapists should ensure that the following factors are considered:

- Priority is given to the best interests of the vulnerable or intimidated witness.
- Impact of therapy upon the conduct of the criminal case needs to be discussed with the witness and their views should be taken into account and may predominate (see below).
- Assessment for possible therapy may require more than one interview to determine if, and in what way, the witness is emotionally disturbed and whether this particular problem can best be helped by the provision of therapy.
- When assessing witnesses with special needs, particular care needs to be taken where the witness has physical or learning difficulties, hearing or speech difficulties and the need for an interpreter, where the native tongue of the witness is not English.

The guidance stresses that some people who have been intimidated or physically beaten and some severely emotionally disturbed people are more likely to produce erroneous or ambiguous responses to leading questions from interviewers, than are less vulnerable people. Therefore, when carrying out an assessment for therapy at the pre-trial stage, therapists should ensure that they use short, plain words, do not ask convoluted, hypothetical or leading questions, use open-ended questions wherever possible and ensure that the witness has understood the questions (Home Office et al., 2001: para 8.1 to 9.6).

The definition of 'vulnerable' in the context of 'vulnerable witnesses' carries specific legal meanings. Adult witnesses may be deemed to be vulnerable if the court considers that the quality of evidence given by the witness is likely to be diminished because:

- The witness suffers from mental disorder within the meaning of the Mental Health Act 1983 or otherwise has a significant impairment of intelligence and social functioning; **or**
- the witness has a physical disability or is suffering from a physical disorder (Youth Justice and Criminal Evidence Act 1999, section 16).

Whether vulnerable or intimidated witnesses should receive therapy before a criminal trial is not a decision for the police or the Crown Prosecution Service or the Procurator Fiscal Service (although whenever practicable they should be consulted before commencing therapy). Such decisions can only be taken by the vulnerable or intimidated witness, in conjunction with the professionals from the agencies providing the service to the witness.

Special measures for vulnerable or intimidated witnesses

In addition to enhancing the possibility of adequate support for vulnerable and intimidated witnesses, new procedures – known as 'special measures' – have been introduced within the courts to assist these witnesses to give evidence. The 'special measures' implemented as a result of the Youth Justice and Criminal Evidence Act 1999 apply to the groups mentioned above and include possibility of:

- Screening the witness from the accused.
- Giving evidence by live television link.
- Removal of wigs and gowns in court.
- Video-recorded evidence-in-chief (questioned by their own solicitor).
- Video recorded cross-examination.
- Examination through an intermediary (see below, last paragraph).
- Clearing the public gallery.
- Provision of aids to communication.
- Greater protection for rape victims, with a ban on victims being cross-examined by the defendant in person and further restrictions on the cross-examination of the victim's sexual history.

In Scotland, similar measures will be put in place by means of the Vulnerable Witnesses (Scotland) Act 2004 when it comes into force.

Successful legal cases have already followed the introduction of these special measures, including a case in which a man was jailed for five years for indecent assault, after his victim, a disabled woman with multiple sclerosis, gave evidence to a jury via a live TV link from her nursing home bed. The conviction represents the first successful outcome of a case involving the special measures under the Youth Justice and Criminal Evidence Act 1999 (www.publicnet.co.uk/publicnet/fe030404.htm).

Other measures with a view to enabling individuals to be comfortable in the court environment have also been introduced. These include pre-court familiarisation visits, the presence of a supporter in court, escorts to and from court, liaison officers, separate waiting areas and the use of pagers. The Home Office reviewed the special measures in 2004 and found that those who used them were less likely to feel stressed or anxious. As therapists working with these victims, it is crucial to be aware of the existence of such measures, as it is this information that may enable victims who are unlikely to come forward to be supported by the 'special measures.' The victim may also choose their therapist to support them after they have given their evidence in court.

The first scheme to help vulnerable witnesses of crime with communication difficulties to give evidence is currently being piloted in Merseyside. The scheme is also due to be piloted in other areas of the country before being implemented on a national scale if successful. Pilots will run until summer 2005 when recommendations will be made for further implementation. The scheme involves a communication expert, such as a speech and language therapists being employed to act as an intermediary to help a witness with communication difficulties. Through this additional support the witness will understand any questions asked and will be able to give their answers in a way that can be understood by the police, judge, legal representatives and the jury. A register of 45 intermediaries has now been established (www.crimereduction.gov.uk/victims31.htm). A helper or therapist may be better placed than the victim to inquire about the availability of local support services. This type of information may be obtained through the courts or witness support.

The overall changes in policy and guidance represent an attempt to redress the balance between defendants and victims. The Department of Constitutional Affairs (2004) has continued to push forward these trends by arguing that people require sufficient confidence in the justice system in order for that system to respond more adequately with crime and anti-social behaviour. Victims, witnesses and jurors have to be central to, and at the heart of, the criminal justice system. This means that the rights of the most vulnerable, including children, victims of domestic violence and the mentally incapable, need to be protected.

Conclusion

Therapeutic practice appears to be lagging behind the recent developments in the law, designed to increase the availability of therapy prior to the court appearance of witnesses, especially victims and those who are vulnerable or intimidated. This is dangerous to clients who may ultimately suffer the consequences in the outcome of the case due to ill-informed or poorly prepared therapists. There may also be a significant waste of public funds in criminal cases or the client's own resources in civil cases when cases collapse unnecessarily due to a therapist's failure to anticipate the potential areas of conflict between providing therapy and the quality of evidence required in a court case. We found sufficient anecdotal accounts to suggest that some therapists may be inadvertently and unnecessarily neglecting this aspect of moving between the therapy room to the court room. Table 7.2 provides a summary of the actions to be taken by the therapist in circumstances where they find themselves involved with working with potential witnesses. Complications arising from poorly conceived therapy with potential witnesses are not just a problem for individual therapists but for their professional bodies as representatives of therapy collectively. Failure to have undertaken adequate preparation prior to supporting witnesses that subsequently leads to complications in litigation diminishes the public reputation of therapists as a whole. Therapists working in statutory services are often better supported and may have access to specialised legal advice and support. Practitioners working outside statutory services may be less well-supported and may have less prior knowledge of the potential areas of difficulty. It may seem rather a large step into unfamiliar territories of practice to contact a law officer or to encourage clients to do so on their own behalf prior to therapy starting. For someone who has not done so before, it can be a scary step into unfamiliar professional relationships. However, the anecdotal evidence is that most law officers are appreciative of being approached in advance of therapy starting and take the initial approach as an indication of a concern about professional standards in a complex professional area of practice. They appear to welcome a realistically cautious approach as an appropriate step towards minimising potential areas of difficulty. Good practice at this point provides a sound starting point to resisting any future accusations of 'coaching' in court, that if established, could be damaging to both the client's and therapist's contributions as witnesses in the case.

Table 7.2   Steps to be taken before counselling potential witnesses

In order to avoid undermining your client's credibility in forthcoming court proceedings:

- Explain the implications of receiving therapy prior to court proceedings to your client and seek your client's permission to take the necessary steps to maximise the therapeutic support available without compromising any future court cases.
- In the case of possible *criminal* cases:

  o   If the offence has not been reported to the police but the client intends to do so, it would be legally better to support the client in reporting the offence and enabling the police to take a full statement before commencing therapy.
  o   Obtain current guidance on providing therapy to witnesses from appropriate web sites.
  o   Before therapy starts discuss with the police and/or the Crown Prosecution Service how therapy will be provided prior to trial.
  o   If therapy has already commenced prior to any knowledge that a trial might take place, inform the police or the Crown Prosecution Service at the earliest possible opportunity. This is potentially a more problematic situation than negotiating the methods and boundaries of therapy in advance.
  o   Anticipate being asked to give evidence in person as a witness to fact and prepare to give evidence in a professional manner appropriate to a legal environment.

- In the case of possible *civil* proceedings:

  o   Ask clients to discuss the possibility of therapy with their lawyers and any safeguards required to avoid undermining their case.
  o   Be prepared for the possibility of being asked to provide a witness of fact report, submitting case records or being asked to appear as a witness.

- In the case of possible *family* court proceedings:

  o   Seek the permission of the court prior to undertaking therapy with anyone who has a significant role in the care or custody of children or young people that are subject to court proceedings.
  o   Be prepared for the possibility of being asked to provide a witness report or, in suitable circumstances, an expert witness report and to appear in person in the court.

- In *all* types of cases, restrict the therapeutic methods and subject matter to ones that minimise the risk of accusations of 'coaching'. Guidance will normally have been given at the point of consultation with the relevant court or law officer. If in doubt, ask.
- If you are not already keeping notes, you must start to *keep brief factual records* of time and duration, people present and topics of therapy sessions.

In the next chapter, we turn our attention to clients applying for criminal compensation. Although a compensation award can never be a full recompense for any suffering caused by a crime or negligence, it can help some clients, and for some it is a significant help, both practically and psychologically.

8

Criminal Compensation

How will therapists encounter this aspect of law in their work?

Compensation is available to individuals or groups of people who suffer a personal injury arising out of crime or negligence on the part of another. In cases of victims of crime, the Criminal Injuries Compensation Authority (CICA) is the public body that administers the criminal injuries compensation scheme throughout England, Scotland and Wales. It has existed since 1964 and deals with applications for compensation from victims of violent crime or those injured trying to apprehend criminals or prevent a crime.

Events leading to a claim may have involved experiences of stress, depression and trauma, for which victims may have been receiving therapy. Therapists may assist a child or adult client seeking compensation for past abuse and any loss of earnings suffered as a consequence of that abuse. They can refer them to the Criminal Injury Compensation Scheme as a means of gaining some remedy for the crime committed against them. A solicitor acting for the client may request a report from the therapist in support of a CICA claim.

Therapists need to be aware that the actual process of obtaining compensation can be laborious and prolonged. A strong support network for the client is therefore crucial when deciding to initiate a claim, as undergoing a legal process such as this could lead to more psychological harm to the client if it does not succeed. An awareness of the claims procedure will mean that you can refer clients to this scheme and gain guidance with regard to writing reports for Criminal Injury Compensation Claim cases from CICA. See Chapter 3 for guidance on writing a report for the CICA.

What does the scheme cover?

Criminal Injuries Compensation is available for abuse committed after 1964, where it can be regarded as an act of violence. Applications are determined on the basis of evidence obtained from applicants, the police, medical bodies and others, such as witnesses to the incident. An independent Criminal Injuries Compensation Authority Panel adjudicates cases where the applicant is not satisfied with the Authority's decision, usually through an oral hearing.

Applications made before 1 April 1996 were based on a different scheme. The applicant's case was assessed on the same basis as for a personal injury claim in the civil courts. In 1996 the system was changed with the introduction of a tariff of injuries. This is now a list of fixed compensation payments for each injury. Although the 1996 scheme was changed again in 2001, the new scheme continues to use a tariff of injuries. CICA is responsible for operating the scheme but not for the rules that it contains. The schemes are made under an act of parliament called the Criminal Injuries Compensation Act 1995.

The CICA scheme applies to all applications received on or after 1 April 2001. It allows financial awards to be made:

- To recognise the injuries, physical or mental, caused by violent crime.
- In certain circumstances to compensate for past or future lost earnings or special expenses caused by such a crime.
- For bereavement as a result of a crime of violence, including in some cases, compensation for surviving dependants, for lost earnings of the person who has been killed.

How can clients make an application under the criminal injuries compensation scheme?

1. The client should submit a completed application form, which will be acknowledged and a personal reference number allocated.
2. The Authority will then make enquiries from the police, doctors and hospitals and any other organisation and people with relevant information about the claim. This may also include the victim's counsellor/therapist. In this initial stage of the enquiry process, the approach adopted by the CICA is to seek a report from therapists in a standard pro forma. An example of the format of such a report is shown at the end of this chapter.
3. Once the enquiries referred to at Stage 2 are completed and all the necessary information has been gathered, the case is allocated to a caseworker. The caseworker will subsequently make a decision about whether or not to accept the application. If it is accepted he or she will provide the victim/client with their contact name and number.
4. After the acknowledgement time is spent on making enquiries; it is here that there may be a significant delay. The waiting time varies depending on how long therapists, police, doctors and hospitals take to provide reports. Further information from these individuals may well be requested, for example, if an opinion requires further clarification.
5. When the caseworker has made all the relevant enquiries, the findings are submitted to a more senior claims officer. This officer is responsible for assessing the claim on the basis of the scheme and whether an award should be made; if so, the amount and how it should be paid. Upon making the decision, claims officers inform clients or their representatives in writing. Where an award is refused or reduced, reasons are given for this.

If the client's offender has been identified and brought to trial, the CICA will wait for the verdict in the case before deciding upon the application for compensation. There are two reasons for this:

- There is a danger that it may be seen to be prejudging the trial verdict if a compensation award is made or refused before the trial is concluded.
- Issues may arise at the trial that could be relevant to the compensation claim. Hence it would be wrong to settle the claim without knowing about such matters.

Special arrangements for paying awards

Account is taken of the circumstances of the victim and any other relevant issues, for example, if the victim is a child or if there is a risk that any award paid to his or her parents would not be used for the child's benefit. A trust may be set up to safeguard the child's interests in these circumstances. A more senior officer within the Authority may review this decision.

Review Procedure

1. Applicants are sent a review form and a guide to review procedures when the original decision is issued.
2. To contest the review decision, clients are entitled to appeal to the Criminal Injuries Compensation Appeals Panel, which is independent of the Authority.

CICA Objective

CICA aims to provide a decision in 90% of cases within 12 months of receiving the application on whether or not the client is eligible for an award, and if eligible, indicating the amount of the award. Criminal trials and cases involving future loss of earnings and future medical expenses generally take longer than a year to settle.

In comparison to a civil court action, the CICA scheme is usually inexpensive, with most applications being dealt with by post. However, there are complex rules that can restrict a person's entitlement, for example, the victim's own character in terms of previous convictions and conduct at the time of the attack. There are restrictions on claims for loss of earnings and the compensation is often much less than in a civil action. There are 25 levels of compensation for injuries ranging from £1,000 to £250,000 and it is unlikely that any award will be made if there has been a full recovery within 6 weeks.

What are the alternative routes to claiming compensation?

Compensation Order

If the perpetrator of a crime is convicted of a criminal offence then the Criminal Court can make a Compensation Order. The police usually provide victims with a form to complete for this. It is a simple scheme that does not cost anything. However, there is no right to an award and, if it is made, it is often for a token amount of a few hundred pounds. If the offender has no means to pay or is sent to prison, it is unlikely that an award will be made.

Civil Court Action

An assault is not only a criminal offence but can also be the basis for a claim for compensation, like any other type of injury. There does not have to be a criminal conviction, as long as the assailant is identified and there is sufficient evidence of the assault. If the case is successful, then the compensation awarded is assessed in the same way as any other injury case. However:

- Unless the perpetrator has means or assets, it is not worth making a claim.
- A full separate civil court case may be needed. This can take time, with the victim experiencing more trauma. It can also be expensive with uncertainty about the outcome. This may involve not only losing the case, but paying the legal costs of the other side.

It is possible to make a claim through all three routes (compensation order, civil courts and CICA) but there can be no 'double recovery'. The CICA deducts any other compensation paid from its award and the Civil Court deducts any payments received under a Compensation Order.

Chapter summary

- Therapists can assist their clients who are victims of crime by referring them to the CICA claim and/or writing a report for them in support of a compensation application.
- It is necessary to make an assessment of the circumstances of the case, and issues of dual relationships and competency need to be addressed as part of that assessment process.
- If you decide to write a report, it is good practice to confirm the content of the report with the client beforehand in order to identify any conflicting views on the harm and impact suffered by the client.
- The CICA scheme is for those who have been physically or mentally injured, or both, as a result of a violent crime. The injury must have happened while the client was in Great Britain (England, Scotland or Wales) and must also be serious enough to qualify for the minimum tariff award.
- Compensation is also available to close relatives and/or dependants if someone has died as a result of a criminal injury.
- Awareness of the criteria for eligibility will enable therapists to assist their clients when they are referring them to agencies that can help victims.
- To apply clients need to:

  (a) Select the type of award.
  (b) Check eligibility.
  (c) Gather the information that is required.
  (d) Complete an application form.

- Awareness of alternative routes to claiming compensation may be helpful but the CICA scheme appears to be the most inexpensive and convenient.
- Therapists can obtain more information about the scheme from the CICA or they can refer to the website at www.cica.gov.uk, where a copy of 'A Guide to the Criminal Injuries Compensation Scheme' is also available.

Example of the standard pro forma report which is sent out in the initial stages of a CICA investigation.

Incident details:

Place:

Date:

Date of first treatment:

Reference number:

Name of injured person:

---

1. Please give details of any physical injuries, treatment given, and any recognised condition resulting from the incident.

| |
| |
| |
| |
| |

Date of first visit _____ Date of last visit _____ No. of visits _____

2. In your opinion has the applicant made a substantial recovery? **Yes/No**
   If **yes**, how long did the main effects last?

| |
| |

3. If **no**, do you expect the applicant to make a substantial recovery in the future? **Yes/No**
   If so, what is the approximate timescale?

| |
| |

4. Please give details of any likely continuing disability or residual scarring.

5. Is the applicant still receiving treatment from you for these injuries (including psychological injuries?)
    Yes/No

6. For how long (in weeks) was the applicant certified unfit for work as a direct result of the injuries?

7. Has the injury accelerated or exacerbated an existing condition? **Yes/No**
    If so:

    (a) what percentage is attributable to acceleration or exacerbation?

    (b) how long did any exacerbation last?

8. Is the applicant receiving treatment from anyone else for these injuries? **Yes/No**
    If **yes,** please give the names and addresses.

9. Please attach **copies of any letters and reports** from A&E units, consultants and other practitioners about the applicant's injuries.
10. Do you have any additional information that would be helpful to us?

Name:_____   **Professional status:**_____

Main employment address: _____

                            _____

                            _____

Signature: _____

Date: _____

Overview of the UK Legal Systems

One of the challenges which therapists face is finding their way around the complex structure that is the courts system of England, Wales and Scotland. This section of the book is useful as a quick reference point for therapists to familiarise themselves with the key roles in the legal field and the structure of the court system. The chapter provides you with sufficient information, mostly in table format, to enable you to find your way around the English, Welsh and Scottish legal systems.

Distinguishing between solicitors and barristers

Therapists are most likely to come into contact with solicitors. They are the general practitioners of the legal system. They are the first point of contact for most individuals or organisations seeking legal advice. Most solicitors work in group practices either as partners or as salaried employees. Solicitors' fees include a substantial amount for the practice overheads and support staff. The training to become a solicitor consists of a law degree, one-year postgraduate legal practice course and two years paid placement in a solicitor's office. In England, the Law Society regulates solicitors through the Office for Supervision of Solicitors and solicitors are required to adhere to the Solicitors Practice Rules and Regulations. If therapists want to find a solicitor they can use the Law Society's own directory Solicitors Online or the Community Legal Service's Advice Search or Directory on their website, Just Ask. The Law Society of Scotland regulates solicitors in a similar way. Therapists can telephone the Law Society for advice in this regard, or use its own directory at www.lawscot.org.uk.

Barristers and advocates

Barristers, known as advocates in Scotland are the consultants of the English and Scottish legal systems. They offer specialised services in giving opinions and advice, and also in representing the client at court. Some have general practices and others specialise in particular areas of the law such as Crime, Family or Personal Injury. A barrister's/advocate's direct access to his or her lay client is very restricted, as it is the solicitor who issues the instructions to act and manages most contacts with clients. All barristers/advocates are sole practitioners, but they gather together to share facilities and expenses, through what is called chambers. In England and Wales, training consists of a law degree, a one-year postgraduate level bar vocational course and one year's placement with a barrister. The General Council of the Bar is the regulatory and representative body for barristers in England and Wales and it has a Code of Conduct to which barristers are required

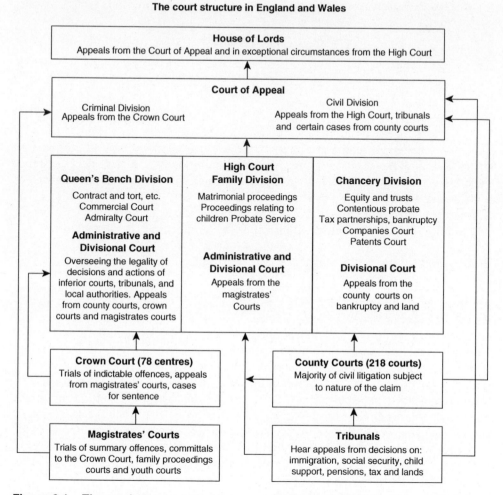

The court structure in England and Wales

House of Lords
Appeals from the Court of Appeal and in exceptional circumstances from the High Court

Court of Appeal

Criminal Division
Appeals from the Crown Court

Civil Division
Appeals from the High Court, tribunals
and certain cases from county courts

High Court

Queen's Bench Division

Contract and tort, etc.
Commercial Court
Admiralty Court

**Administrative and
Divisional Court**

Overseeing the legality of
decisions and actions of
inferior courts, tribunals, and
local authorities. Appeals
from county courts, crown
courts and magistrates courts

Family Division

Matrimonial proceedings
Proceedings relating to
children Probate Service

**Administrative and
Divisional Court**

Appeals from the
magistrates'
Courts

Chancery Division

Equity and trusts
Contentious probate
Tax partnerships, bankruptcy
Companies Court
Patents Court

Divisional Court

Appeals from the
county courts on
bankruptcy and land

Crown Court (78 centres)
Trials of indictable offences, appeals
from magistrates' courts, cases
for sentence

County Courts (218 courts)
Majority of civil litigation subject
to nature of the claim

Magistrates' Courts
Trials of summary offences, committals
to the Crown Court, family proceedings
courts and youth courts

Tribunals
Hear appeals from decisions on:
immigration, social security, child
support, pensions, tax and lands

Figure 9.1   The modern court structure over England and Wales, also available on the court service website.

to adhere. In Scotland training involves a law degree, a one-year postgraduate legal practice course, a one or two year traineeship in a solicitor's office and nine month's placement with an advocate. The Faculty of Advocates is the regulatory and representative body for advocates in Scotland and it has a Code of Conduct to which advocates are required to adhere.

For more information regarding the UK court system visit the court service website at www.courtservice.gov.uk (see Figures 9.1 and 9.2). It carries out administrative and support tasks for the Court of Appeal, the High Court, the Crown Court, the county courts, the Probate Service, and certain tribunals.

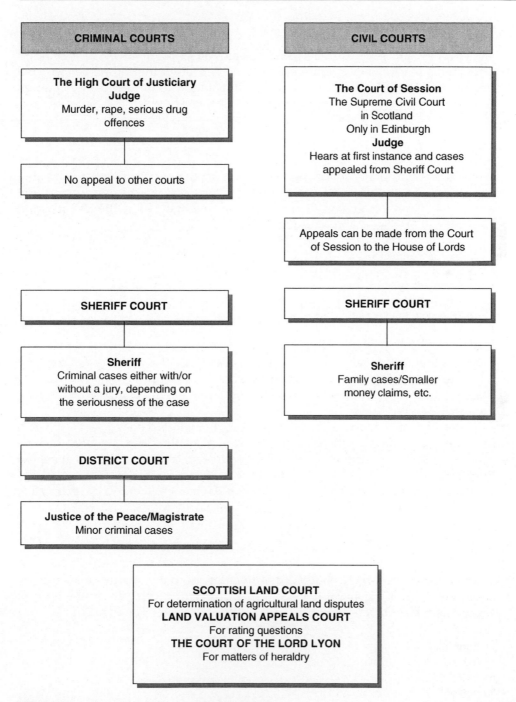

Figure 9.2   The court structure in Scotland

The civil and criminal procedures

The court system is divided between different areas of the law. The significant distinctions that therapists are most likely to encounter are those between civil and criminal law. The examples below are illustrations of the difference between civil and criminal and the types of cases, which come before these courts.

Civil cases

Civil cases are primarily concerned with resolving disputes between citizens and, where appropriate, providing restitution in the form of damages to place the party who has suffered loss in a position comparable to that of before the loss occurred (see Figure 9.3). They include the following:

- breach of contract
- accident
- personal injury
- defamation of character
- professional negligence.

The following are fictional examples of the types of cases heard in the civil courts:

A local therapist is being sued by an ex-client for £50,000 for breach of contract. Ann Smith claims that Sarah Jones breached a term of confidentiality when she shared information she had discussed about her childhood in the counselling room with a fellow colleague.

Sunita Sharma, who suffered serious psychological damage at as a result of receiving negligent advice from her therapist, has been awarded £35,000 compensation for the damage caused. The judgement came after 4 years of intense litigation.

Theresa Jones sues her former client for non-payment of therapy fees. The client is counterclaiming that there was no agreement to pay fees.

Criminal Cases

Criminal cases are largely concerned with enforcing public morals and rules by determining guilt and imposing penalties in the guilty, typically in the form of fines, community orders or imprisonment (see Figure 9.4). These include:

- murder
- manslaughter
- burglary
- assault
- criminal damage.

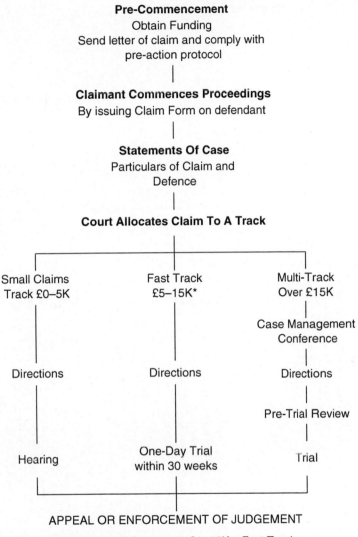

Pre-Commencement
Obtain Funding
Send letter of claim and comply with
pre-action protocol

Claimant Commences Proceedings
By issuing Claim Form on defendant

Statements Of Case
Particulars of Claim and
Defence

Court Allocates Claim To A Track

Small Claims Track £0–5K	Fast Track £5–15K*	Multi-Track Over £15K
		Case Management Conference
Directions	Directions	Directions
		Pre-Trial Review
Hearing	One-Day Trial within 30 weeks	Trial

APPEAL OR ENFORCEMENT OF JUDGEMENT

* in personal injury cases £1–15K = Fast Track

Figure 9.3   An overview of the civil procedure

The following fictional examples are cases that can appear in criminal courts:

Andrew Jones has been sentenced to prison for 15 years after his victim gave evidence against him by live TV link. Thirteen-year-old Manjit Kaur was abused physically on a daily basis by her foster parent.

Mahmood Iqbal has been imprisoned for life after divulging information to her therapist about a pre-planned terrorist attack on a Wessex town centre.

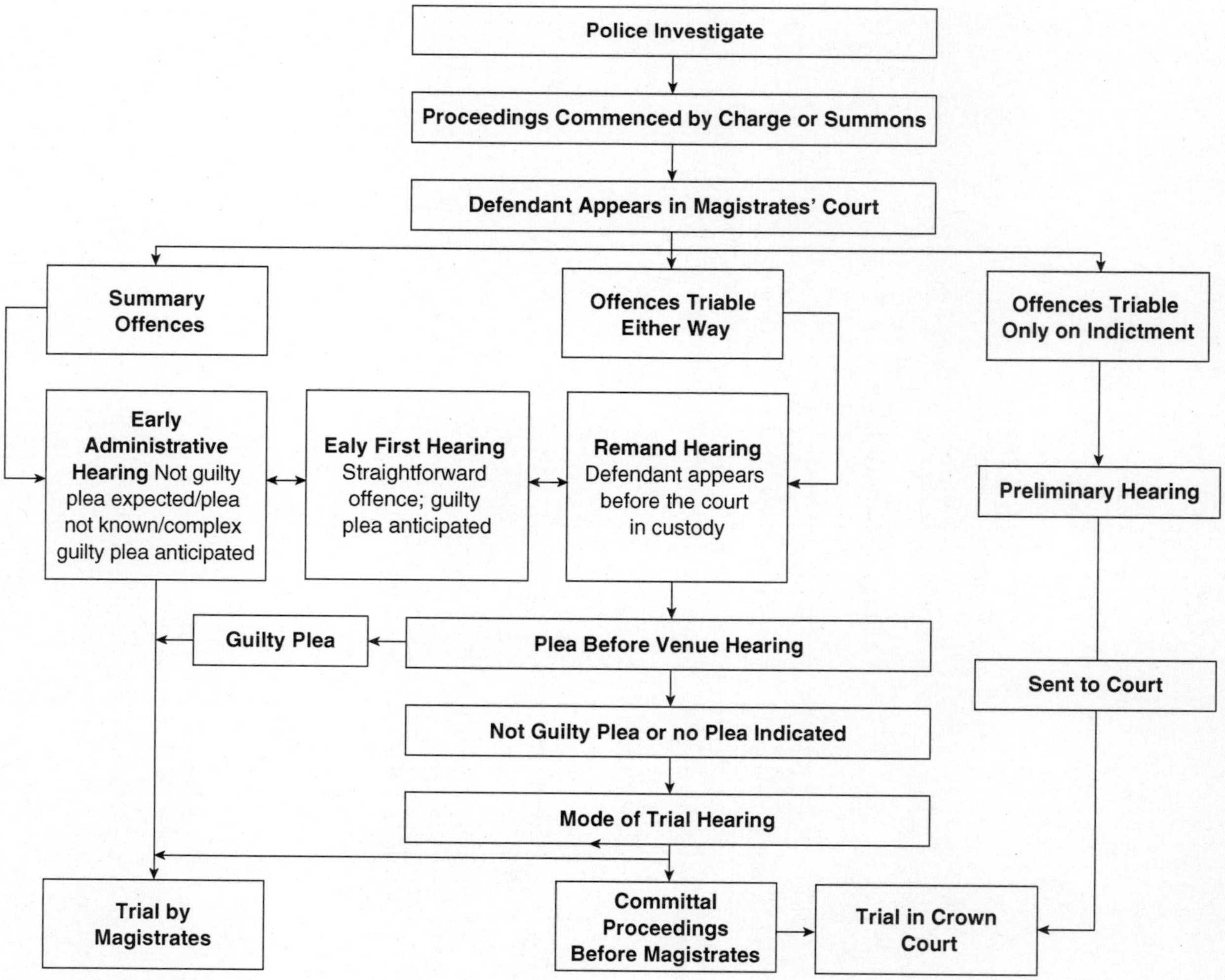

Figure 9.4 An overview of criminal procedure

Claire Brown murders her husband after suffering years of mental and physical abuse. Therapists appear as expert witnesses. They offer the professional opinion that the murder was provoked by years of abuse and mental torture.

Differences between civil and criminal cases

It is a common misconception that you can only be tried once for the consequences of any particular offence. However, this is not the case. It is possible that therapists could become involved with both criminal and civil law with regard to the same matter. Consider the following example:

> A criminal case for sexual assault collapses against an individual and the victim brings a claim for damages in the civil courts.

One incident can lead to a number of different claims and actions. For example, in this case the victim could bring a criminal action in order to seek the punishment of the person alleged to have committed the offence. In civil proceedings, the purpose would be to seek restitution through claiming compensation and damages. In addition to this, the perpetrator of the crime may also face disciplinary hearings at work, as well as professional conduct proceedings by their relevant professional body.

The information in the following table illustrates the significant differences between civil and criminal cases. Table 9.1 is relevant to England and Wales and Table 9.2 applies to Scotland. It will help therapists to see the different ways in which they operate.

Table 9.1 Differences between criminal and civil cases in England and Wales

Criminal Cases	Civil Cases
Parties	*Parties*
The prosecution prosecutes the defendant (often referred to in courts as 'the accused').	The claimant sues the individual.
The prosecution will be conducted by the Crown Prosecution Service.	In divorce cases the parties are petitioner and respondent.
On appeal, technically the parties become appellant and respondent but are often still referred to as before.	On appeal, as for criminal cases.
Which Court?	*Which Court?*
Criminal offences are procedurally classified as follows (Criminal Law Act 1977):	This depends on the track to which the case is allocated (see Figure 9.4).

(Continued)

Table 9.1 (Continued)

Criminal Cases	Civil Cases
• Offences triable on indictment only (e.g. murder and rape). • Offences triable summarily only (e.g. public disorder and motoring offences). • Offences triable either way (e.g. theft).	• Cases that involve a claim for £15,000 or less must be started in the County Court. There is also the option of making a claim through the internet at www.small-claims.co.uk. • In London, the High Court at the Royal Courts of Justice will initially only deal with cases over £15,000 and, ultimately, only those over £50,000.

The Burden of Proof

The burden of proof lies on the prosecution; the defendant is presumed innocent and it is for the prosecution to prove guilt, not for the defendant to prove his innocence.

The Burden of Proof

The burden of proof is on the claimant to prove the elements necessary to establish the defendant's liability. If the claimant does so, the defendant will be liable, unless he is able to establish a defence. The burden of proving a defence lies on the defendant.

The Standard of Proof

The prosecution must prove the defendant's guilt 'beyond reasonable doubt', i.e. the jury or magistrates must be sure that that the defendant is guilty.

The Standard of Proof

The standard of proof is on 'a balance of probabilities', i.e. that one party's account of the facts is more likely to be correct than that offered by the other.

Result

If the defendant is found guilty, he or she is convicted of the offence by, for example, fine, imprisonment or community service order.

Result

If the defendant loses, he or she is neither 'guilty', 'convicted' nor 'sentenced'. She or he is merely said to be 'liable to the claimant'. The judgment may, for example, order the defendant to pay damages, perform his or her obligations under a contract, return goods or desist from a course of conduct.

Appeals

The parties to an appeal are appellant and the respondent.

A defendant can appeal to the Crown Court, the High Court and the criminal division of the Court of Appeal. To appeal to the House of Lords, the defendant must get permission from the Court of Appeal.

Appeals

The parties are appellant and respondent

The main appellate courts are the High Court, the civil division of the Court of Appeal and the House of Lords. As in criminal cases, permission is required to appeal to the House of Lords.

Glossary

Action   The lawful demand of an individual's right. A civil action is brought to enforce a civil right, for instance, if a person seeks to recover money. A penal action aims at some penalty or punishment of the party sued. Criminal actions, for instance prosecutions, are of a public nature, in the name of the Queen, against one or more persons accused of a crime.

Adjudication   The giving of a judgement which leads to a sentence or decision.

Adverse witness   A witness hostile to the party calling him or her, who may, with the leave of the court, cross-examine him or her.

Affirm   To confirm a former law or judgement. For example, a Court of Appeal is said to *affirm* the judgement of the court below. To *affirm* also means to make a solemn declaration, equivalent to a statement upon oath.

Appeal   A complaint to a superior court of an injustice done by an inferior one. The party complaining is called the appellant and the other party is called the respondent.

Arbitration   This is the settling of a dispute by an arbitrator/s. Arbitration is a long-established alternative to litigation (it may not always be less complex) and which involves an arbitrator reaching a judgment that is binding on both parties. Where arbitrators cannot agree they may appoint an 'umpire'. The decision of an arbitrator is known as an 'award'.

Barrister   He or she is a specialist in advocacy, presenting cases in court under instruction from a solicitor.

Breach   For example, a breach of a contract, where there is non-compliance with a contract term. A breach gives rise to a claim for compensation in the civil courts.

Burden of proof   This is the duty of proving one's case. In general the burden of proof lies with the claimant or the prosecution.

Cause of action   The ground or grounds on which an action can be brought.

Chief, examination in   The examination of a witness by the party who calls him or her.

Chambers   All barristers are sole practitioners but they gather together to share facilities and expenses. The place is known as barristers' chambers.

Closed court   This is where restrictions are placed on members of the public and the press to view court proceedings. Family proceedings take place in a closed court.

Common Law   The ancient unwritten law of the United Kingdom. This is the law that is embodied in judicial decisions as opposed to statute law, for example the law enacted by Parliament.

Complainant   One who commences a prosecution, action or claim against another.

Conciliation   A settling of disputes without litigation.

Consent   Giving permission freely. If consent is obtained by fraud or undue influence, it is not valid or binding.

Contempt of court   This is anything that tends to create a disregard of the authority of courts of justice. For example, an open insult or resistance to the judges who preside there, or disobedience to their orders. Contempt of court is punishable by imprisonment of the offender or a fine.

Contract   An agreement enforceable at law made verbally or in writing.

Contributory negligence   Negligence, by which a person contributes to the occurrence of an accident to himself, for which others are partially, or even mainly responsible.

Conviction   An individual, being indicted for a crime, admits it, or having pleaded not guilty, is found guilty by the verdict of a jury. This will lead to some kind of punishment, for example, imprisonment.

Coroner   A coroner is empowered by the state to inquire into the manner of the death of any person who is killed, or dies a violent or unnatural death or a sudden death, the cause of which is unknown, or has died in prison.

Cross-examination   The examination of a witness by the opposing barrister. Leading questions are allowed, which is not the case in examination-in-chief.

Damages   The money awarded by a judge or jury in a civil action for the wrong suffered by the claimant.

Direction to a jury   Where a judge instructs a jury on any point of law so that they can apply it to the facts in evidence before them.

Discovery   (1) Of *facts*, obtainable by either party to an action, in the form of answers on oath to questions. The answers may be submitted as evidence in a trial. (2) Of *documents*, obtained as above. The party against whom an order for discovery of documents is made must submit a form setting out all the documents relating to the action, which are or have been in his possession or power.

Dismissal of action   This may take place if the statement of claim is not submitted or through non-appearance at a trial.

Document   A written paper or something similar which may be put forward as evidence. 'Document' includes, in addition to a document in writing: (a) map, plan, graph, drawing (b) photograph (c) any disc, tape, soundtrack or other data are embodied (d) any film, negative, tape or other device in which one or more visual images are.

Examination   The interrogation of witnesses. The *examination-in-chief* of a witness is the interrogation of a witness, in the first instance, by the legal representative of the party calling him. The examination by the opposing legal representative is known as the cross-examination; and further examination by your own side, on points arising out of the cross-examination, is called the re-examination.

Examiners of the court   Barristers of not less than three years' standing appointed by the Lord Chancellor to examine witnesses out of court.

Expert   A skilled witness called to give evidence in the subject in which he or she is a specialist.

Falsify   To tamper and make something inaccurate, for example, a report, in order to deceive.

Hearing   The trial of an action. In general, all cases, both civil and criminal, must be heard in open court. But in certain exceptional cases, where the administration of justice would be rendered impracticable by the presence of the public, the court may sit in camera, for example, when evidence is given by children or young persons.

Hearsay evidence   Second-hand information that a witness only heard about from someone else and did not see or hear himself. Generally, hearsay is not admitted in court because it's not reliable, though there are many exceptions to this.

Incitement   To provoke another person to commit a crime. If a crime is actually committed, the person inciting becomes an accessory before the fact.

Inquest   An inquisition or inquiry, e.g. coroner's inquest.

Inspection of documents   The right of a party in an action or suit to inspect and take copies of documents material to his or her case, which may be in the possession of the opposite party. With regard to other documents, the party desiring to inspect takes out a summons requiring his or her opponent to state what documents are in their possession, and to fill out the appropriate form for that purpose.

Instruct   To convey information or to give instructions. For example, by a client to a solicitor, or by a solicitor to a barrister; to authorise one to appear as an advocate.

Judge's order   An order made on summons by a Judge in Chambers.

Judgement   The sentence or order of the court in a civil or criminal proceeding.

Legal expenses insurance   Insurance against risks of loss to the insured attributable to his or her incurring legal expenses (including the costs of litigation).

Negligence   Omission of a positive duty. The question of negligence is one of fact for the jury, after the judge has decided that there is evidence from which negligence can be reasonably inferred. In criminal cases it is necessary to prove a higher degree of negligence than in civil cases.

Oath   The law requires an oath for many purposes, for example, before giving evidence as a witness in court.

Offence   An act or omission punishable under the criminal law.

Open court   A court to which the public has access as of right.

Perjury   Lying on oath absolutely and falsely in court proceedings, in a matter that is material to the issue or cause in question.

Pleading   (1) The written pleadings in a suit or action. (2) Advocating a client's cause in court.

Prima facie case   A litigating party is said to have a prima facie case when the evidence in his or her favour is sufficiently strong. His or her opponent is to be called into answer it.

Prosecution   The party by whom criminal proceedings are commenced in a court of justice.

Public interest immunity   The right of the Crown to withhold the disclosure and production of a document on the ground that its disclosure and production would be injurious to the public interest. The court may allow or reject the claim.

Rebutting evidence   Evidence presented to destroy the effect of prior evidence, not only in explaining it away while admitting its truth, but also by direct denial, or by an attack on the credibility of the witness who has given it.

Re-examination   The examination of a witness by the barrister of the party on whose behalf he or she has given evidence, in reference to matters arising out of his or her cross-examination.

Re-hearing   A hearing again of a matter which has been heard previously.

Remedy   The means given by law for the recovery of a right, or of compensation for its infringement.

Search warrant   A warrant granted by a judge or magistrate to search a house, shop, land or other premises.

Striking out pleadings   The court or judge may at any stage of the proceedings make an order to strike out or amend anything in the pleadings which is unnecessary, scandalous, or which tends to embarrass or delay the fair trial of the action.

Subpoena   (1) An order directed to a person commanding him or her, under a penalty, to appear and give evidence. (2) An order directed to a person, requiring him or her not only to give evidence, but to bring with them such deeds or writings as the party who issues the subpoena may think material for his or her purpose.

Summary conviction   A conviction before magistrates without the intervention of a jury.

Summing up   In a civil or criminal trial before a judge and jury, this is the process whereby the judge summarises in greater or lesser detail, the statements of the witnesses and the contents of documents, commenting on the manner in which they bear on the issue, and giving his or her direction on any matter of law which may arise from them.

Summons   (1) An order to appear before a judge or magistrate. (2) An application to a judge at chambers.

Trial   The examination of a cause, civil or criminal, before a judge who has jurisdiction over it, according to the laws of the land.

Undue influence   Any improper pressure put on a person to induce him or her to confer a benefit on the party exercising the pressure.

Verdict   The answer given to the court by the jury in any cause, civil or criminal committed to their trial.

Without prejudice   This is relating to any matter in question so that a decision arrived at, or an action taken, is not to be held to affect such questions but to leave it open. For example, when a solicitor writes on behalf of a client to offer a compromise of a question in dispute, he or she can guard themselves by stating that what they offer is without prejudice to any question in dispute.

Witness   A person who, on oath or solemn affirmation, gives evidence in any cause or matter.

Youth Courts   The Youth Court is a section of the Magistrates Court and can be located in the same building. It deals with almost all cases involving young people under the age of 18. The public are excluded from such courts. The Youth Courts in Scotland deals with 16–17-year-old persistent offenders, with the flexibility to deal with 15-year-olds in certain circumstances.

References

Ball, C., McCormac, K. & Stone, N. (1995). *Young offenders: law, policy and practice*. London: Sweet & Maxwell.

Bond, T. (2002). The law of confidentiality – a solution or part of the problem? In P. Jenkins (Ed.), *Legal issues in counselling and psychotherapy* (pp. 123–143). London: Sage.

Bond, T., Casemore, R., Jones, C. & Shilto-Clarke, C. (2001). Access to case notes. *Counselling & Psychotherapy Journal*, 12(9), 6–8.

Browne, K. & Catlow, M. (2004). *Civil litigation*. Guildford: The College of Law.

Department for Constitutional Affairs (2005). *Disclosure of information in family proceedings cases involving children, a consultation*. Retrieved from www.dca.gov.uk

Dorries, C. (1999). *Coroner's courts: a guide to law and practice*. Chichester: John Wiley & Sons Ltd.

Hamilton, C. (2002). *Working with young people: legal responsibility and liability* (5th edn). London: The Children's Legal Centre.

Hamlyn, B., Phelps, A., Tutle, J. & Sattar, G. (2004). *Are special measures working? Evidence from surveys of vulnerable and intimidated witnesses*. London: Home Office.

Harrison, R. (2000). The impact of stranger murder. *The Therapist*, 6(1), 38.

Home Office (2004). *Victims' charter*. London: Home Office.

Home Office, Crown Prosecution Service and Department of Health (2001). *Provision of therapy for child witnesses prior to a criminal trial – practice guidance*. London: The Stationery Office, also available at www.cps.gov.uk

Home Office, Crown Prosecution Service and Department of Health (2001). *Practice guidance for the provision of therapy prior to a criminal trial for vulnerable or intimidated witnesses*, also available at www.cps.gov.uk

Interdepartmental Working Group (1998). *Report of the Interdepartmental Working Group on the treatment of vulnerable or intimidated witnesses in the Criminal Justice System*. London: Home Office.

Jenkins, P., Stone, J. & Keter, V. (2004). *Psychotherapy and the law, questions & answers for counsellors and therapists*. London: Whurr Publishers Ltd.

Morgan, J. & Zedner, L. (1992). *Child victims: crime, impact, and criminal justice*. Oxford: Clarendon Press.

Pattenden, R. (2003). *The law of professional-client confidentiality*. Oxford: Oxford University Press.

Pollecoff, P. (2002). Reports and presenting evidence in court: a guide for counsellors and psychotherapists. In P. Jenkins (Ed.), *Legal issues in counselling and psychotherapy* (pp. 57–51). London: Sage.

Scottish Executive (2003). *Interviewing child witnesses in Scotland*, available at www.scotland.gov.uk

Scottish Executive (2005). *Code of practice to facilitate the provision of therapeutic support to child witnesses in court proceedings*, available at www.scotland.gov.uk

Shepherd, J. (1997). Victims of violent crime. *Accident and Emergency Nursing*, 6(1), 15–17.

Shepherd, J. (1998). Tackling violence: interagency procedures and injury surveillance are urgently needed. *British Medical Journal*, *316*, 879–880, also available at http://bmj.bmjjournals.com/cgi/content/full/316/7135/879 (accessed 20/05/2005).

Smith Landsman, I. (2002). Crises of meaning in trauma and loss. In J. Kauffman (Ed.), *Loss of the assumptive world: a theory of traumatic loss* (pp. 13–30). New York: Brunner-Routledge.

Spencer, J. R. (1992). Reforming the law on children's evidence in England. In H. Dent & R. Flin (Eds), *Children as witnesses* (pp. 113–129). Chichester: Wiley.

Victim Support (2002). *No justice beyond criminal justice*. London: Victim Support.

Victims' Voice (2002). *Sudden death and the coroner*. Chippenham: Victims' Voice.

Williams, B. (2002). Counselling in legal settings: provision for jury members, vulnerable witnesses and victims of crime. In P. Jenkins (Ed.), *Legal Issues in Counselling and Psychotherapy* (pp. 105–122). London: Sage.

Yule, W., Perrin, S. & Smith, P. (1999). Post-traumatic stress disorders in children and adolescents. In W. Yule (Ed.), *Post-traumatic stress disorders: concepts and therapy* (pp. 25–50). Chichester: Wiley.

Useful internet sites

For more information regarding confidentiality refer to *NHS Confidentiality Code of Practice*: www.dh.gov.uk/PublicationsAndStatistics

Home Office website:
www.crimereduction.gov.uk

I have been asked to be a witness – what do I do?
Retrieved 6 February 2005 from:
www.courtservice.gov.uk/using_courts/witness/index.htm

Instructing expert witnesses: guidelines for solicitors
Retrieved 9 February 2005 from:
www.theexpertwitnessdirectory.co.uk/guidelines.htm

Guidelines for applying for compensation under the Criminal Injuries Compensation Scheme.
Retrieved 16 January 2005 from:
www.cica.gov.uk

Victims and Witnesses, *Easing Communication for Vulnerable Witnesses*
Retrieved 3 February 2005 from:
www.crimereduction.gov.uk/victims31.htm

A review into the needs of vulnerable or intimidated witnesses: measures in Youth Justice and Criminal Evidence Act 1999.
Retrieved 6 February 2005 from:
www.publicnet.co.uk/publicnet/fe030404.htm

Witnesses in the Civil Courts and Witnesses in the Crown Court
Retrieved 9 February, 2005 from:
www.courtservice.gov.uk/using_courts/witness/index.htm

UK Litigation & Dispute Resolution Law articles in association with Wragge & Co. *Pre-action disclosure – substantive claim only has to be properly arguable.*
Retrieved 16 January 2005 from:
www.legal500.com/devs/uk/lt/uklt_177.htm

Scottish Courts
www.scotcourts.gov.uk

References to legal cases cited in the text

Barclays Bank plc v. *O'Brien* [1994] 1 AC 180
Beck v. *Ministry of Defence* [2003] EWCA Civ 1043 [2003]
Devoran Joinery Co Ltd v. *Perkins* (No. 2) [2003] EWCA Civ 1241 [2003]
Durant v. *Financial Services Authority* [2003] EWCA Civ 1746, CA
Lucas v. *Barking, Havering and Redbridge Hospitals NHS Trust* [2003] EWCA Civ 1102 [2004]
R. v. *Sinha, The Times*, 13 July 1994
Re J [1991] FCR 191 at 226/7
Re L (a minor) (police investigation) [1996] 2 WLR 395, HL
Re R (a minor: expert's evidence (note)) [1991] 1 FLR 291 Cazalet J
Rose v. *Lynx Express Ltd and Bridgepoint Capital (Nominees) Ltd* [2004] EWCA Civ 447
W v. *Egdell and Others* [1990] Ch 359 1 All ER 835
Wardlaw v. *Farrar* [2003] EWCA Civ 1719 [2003]
Youssef v. *Jordan* [2003] EWCA Civ 1852 *Times*, 22 January 2004

Acts and Rules cited in the text

Administration of Justice Act 1960
Administration of Justice (Scotland) Act 1972
Children Act 1989
Children Act 2004
Children (Scotland) Act 2005
Civil Procedure Rules 1998
The Civil Procedure Rules, Professional Negligence Pre-action Protocol, Part B Coroners Act 1988
Coroners Court Rules 1984
County Courts Act 1984
County Court Rules 1981
Criminal Injuries Compensation Act 1995
Criminal Justice Act 1967
Data Protection Act 1998
Fatal Accidents and Sudden Deaths Inquiry (Scotland) Act 1976
Freedom of Information Act 2000
Mental Health Act 1983
Supreme Court Act 1981
Vulnerable Witnesses (Scotland) Act 2004
Youth Justice and Criminal Evidence Act 1999

Index